WALKING ON THE
ISLE OF ARRAN

About the Author

Paddy Dillon is a prolific outdoor writer with over 30 guidebooks to his name, as well as more than a dozen booklets and brochures. He writes for outdoor magazines and other publications, as well as for tourism organisations.

Paddy lives near the Lake District and has walked in every county in England, Scotland, Ireland and Wales, writing about walks in every one of them. Paddy enjoys simple day walks, challenging long-distance walks, and is a dedicated island-hopper. He has led guided walks and walked extensively in Europe, as well as in Nepal, Tibet, Africa and the Rocky Mountains of Canada and the USA.

While researching routes, Paddy inputs his information directly onto a palmtop computer so that his descriptions are precise, having been written at the very point at which the reader will need them. Paddy takes his own photographs, has appeared on radio and TV, and is a member of the Outdoor Writers' Guild.

Other Cicerone guides by Paddy Dillon include:

South West Coast Path
Channel Island Walks
Irish Coastal Walks
The Irish Coast to Coast Walk
The Mountains of Ireland
Walking in County Durham
Walking in the Galloway Hills
Walking in the North Pennines
GR20: Corsica – the High Level Route

Walking in Madeira
Walking in the Canary Islands – West
Walking in the Canary Islands – East
Walking in Malta
The Cleveland Way and the Yorkshire
 Wolds Way
The North York Moors
Walking in the Isles of Scilly

WALKING ON THE ISLE OF ARRAN

by

Paddy Dillon

2 POLICE SQUARE, MILNTHORPE, CUMBRIA LA7 7PY
www.cicerone.co.uk

© Paddy Dillon 1998, 2006
First edition 1998, ISBN 1 85284 269 5, reprinted 2003
Second edition 2006
ISBN-10: 1-85284-478-7
ISBN-13: 978-1-85284-478-3

British Library Cataloguing–in-Publication Data
A catalogue record for this book is available from the British Library.

OS Ordnance Survey® This product includes mapping data licensed from Ordnance Survey® with the permission of the Controller of Her Majesty's Stationery Office. © Crown copyright 2002. All rights reserved. Licence number PU100012932

All photograph

Advice to Readers

Readers are advised that while every effort is taken by the author to ensure the accuracy of this guidebook, changes can occur which may affect the contents. It is advisable to check locally on transport, accommodation, shops, etc, but even rights of way can be altered. Paths can be affected by forestry work, landslip or changes of ownership.

The author would welcome information on any updates and changes sent through the publishers.

Front cover: Walkers pick a way round a granite tor between North Goat Fell and Goat Fell (Walk 41)

CONTENTS

Warning

Mountain walking can be a dangerous activity carrying a risk of personal injury or death. It should be undertaken only by those with a full understanding of the risks and with the training and/or experience to evaluate them. Whilst every care and effort has been taken in the preparation of this book, the user should be aware that conditions can be highly variable and can change quickly, thus materially affecting the seriousness of a mountain walk.

Therefore, except for any liability which cannot be excluded by law, neither Cicerone nor the author accepts liability for damage of any nature (including damage to property, personal injury or death) arising directly or indirectly from the information in this book.

To call out the **rescue services**, phone 999 or the European emergency number 112. Once connected to the emergency operator, ask for the police, ambulance, fire service, coastguard or mountain rescue, as appropriate. Give them your contact details and remain in touch to await further instructions.

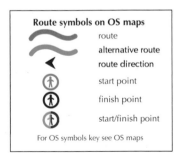

Route symbols on OS maps

route

alternative route

route direction

start point

finish point

start/finish point

For OS symbols key see OS maps

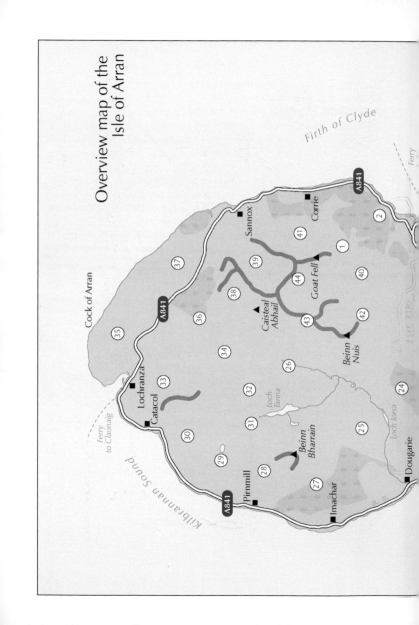

Overview map of the
Isle of Arran

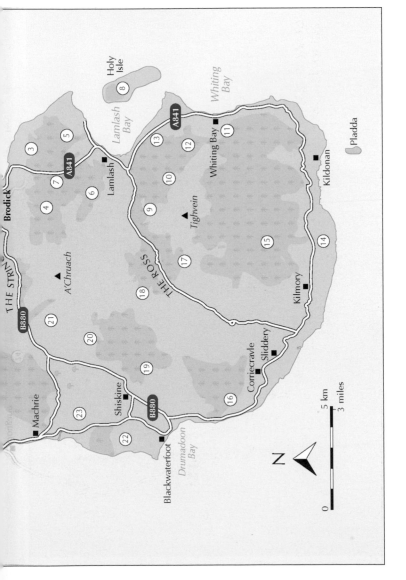

THE STRIN[G]

Brodick

B880

A'Chruach ▲

THE ROSS

Machrie ■

Shiskine ■

B880

Blackwaterfoot

Drumadoon Bay

Corriecravie
Sliddery ■

Kilmory ■

Kildonan ■

Pladda

Holy Isle

Lamlash Bay

Lamlash ■

A841

Whiting Bay

Whiting Bay ■

A841

Tighvein ▲

③ ④ ⑤ ⑥ ⑦ ⑧ ⑨ ⑩ ⑪ ⑫ ⑬ ⑭ ⑮ ⑯ ⑰ ⑱ ⑲ ⑳ ㉑ ㉒ ㉓

N

0   5 km
    3 miles

Craggy Cir Mhòr and Goat Fell as seen from the 'dress circle' on Caisteal Abhail (Walk 39)

INTRODUCTION

The Isle of Arran rises proudly from the Firth of Clyde between Ayrshire and Kintyre. Its mountainous form dominates the open waters of the Clyde and its jagged peaks present a great challenge to walkers. People first came to the island some 5500 years ago, though some periods of its history are but dimly recorded. Tourism has been important for little more than the past century. The Isle of Arran has much to offer the visitor and is often described as 'Scotland in miniature'. Roads are very few, but opportunities to explore the island on foot are many and varied. This guidebook offers a selection of 45 walks, and as many of them are interlinked, there are opportunities to create longer walks traversing the length and breadth of the island.

GETTING TO THE ISLE OF ARRAN

Although some people imagine it is more difficult to travel to an island than it is to travel to a mainland destination, travel to the Isle of Arran is remarkably easy. The island is close to Glasgow; a very important transport hub with busy road and rail services and nearby international airports. Onward connections to the Isle of Arran are swift and frequent.

By Air: The nearest practical airports are Glasgow International Airport and Prestwick International Airport; the latter handling budget flights from around Europe and enjoying good bus and rail services into Glasgow for onward connections. There is no airport on the Isle of Arran, but there is the option of chartering a helicopter flight from Glasgow or Prestwick airports to the island. Contact Arran Heli-Tours for a quote, ☎ 01770 860526 or 860326.

By Rail: Comfortable long-distance Virgin Trains services start from points as distant as London Euston, Birmingham, Brighton, Bournemouth and Penzance, then run northwards through Britain to converge on Glasgow Central Station. Timetables and fares can be checked, and bookings made, at **www.virgintrains.co.uk**. SPT runs trains from Glasgow Central Station to Ardrossan Harbour, taking 55 minutes and linking with ferries to the Isle of Arran. Check train timetables at **www.spt.co.uk**. When you buy rail tickets, the ferry journey to Brodick on the Isle of Arran can be included in the price.

By Bus: National Express coaches (www.nationalexpress.co.uk) run from many points around Britain, along with Scottish Citylink coaches (www.citylink.co.uk) to converge on Buchanan Street bus station in Glasgow. Stagecoach Western Scotland buses operate from Buchanan Street Bus Station to Ardrossan, and the same company also operates bus services around the Isle of Arran (www.stage-coachbus.com/western).

By Car: Driving from Glasgow, the following roads could be used to reach Ardrossan: the coastal A78 via Largs; the A737 via Beith; or the A736 via Irvine. Drivers from Northern Ireland who arrive at Stranraer simply follow the A77 and A78 main coastal road. Drivers from England should leave the M6 and follow the A75 and A76 for a scenic approach to Ardrossan through the Southern Uplands. Drivers coming from Western Scotland can avoid travelling through Glasgow by following the A83 road onto Kintyre, then use the summer ferry service from Claonaig to Lochranza on the Isle of Arran.

By Ferry: Caledonian MacBrayne (www.calmac.co.uk) operate four, five or six sailings per day between Ardrossan Harbour and Brodick throughout the year, with a typical journey time of 55 minutes. There is also a summer ferry service between Claonaig on the Kintyre peninsula, and Lochranza on the Isle of Arran, taking only 30 minutes. Both ferries carry vehicles.

GETTING AROUND THE ISLE OF ARRAN

All public transport services on the Isle of Arran, including bus services and ferries, with some mainland connections, are contained in a single timetable booklet specially produced for use on the island (this can be obtained from the Brodick Tourist Information Centre in advance of your trip – see Appendix 2 for address details). Take note of the slight variations in services between schooldays and school holidays, as well as Saturdays and Sundays. It is worth mentioning that this entire book was researched and updated exclusively using local bus services. Walkers should realise that there is no need to take a vehicle onto the Isle of Arran – almost every place that could be reached by car is also served by buses. Walking clubs from the mainland are regular weekend users of the buses.

By Stagecoach Bus: Starting from the ferry terminal at Brodick, Stagecoach Western Scottish buses (www.stage-coachbus.com/western), run around the Isle of Arran from early in the morning until late at night. Typically, buses start soon after 0600 and run until 2100, with some services running almost to 2330 on Fridays.

The Isle of Arran has an excellent bus service
that reaches the starting point of most walks

There are slight seasonal variations, and Sunday services are less frequent than weekdays. Several buses run between Brodick, Lamlash and Whiting Bay, which are the three largest villages on Arran. Buses also run back and forth along the B880 String Road, between Brodick and Blackwaterfoot. A service running round the northern half of the island is complimented by another service running round the southern half of the island. Together, these buses cover a complete circuit around the coastal A841 road, linking all the villages. Arran Rural Rover tickets are remarkably cheap and offer a whole day's unlimited travel around the island. In the summer months, Stagecoach operate a number of special services, including an open-top bus between Brodick and Whiting Bay, and a veteran coach service from Brodick to Brodick Castle. There are also half-day and full-day island tours, which don't need to be booked, but run with whatever passengers turn up each day.

By Postbus: The only road not served by Stagecoach buses is The Ross, a minor road running from Lamlash to Sliddery via Glenscorrodale. This road has a twice daily Postbus service, except Sundays. There are also two Postbus services each day, except Sundays, around the northern and southern halves of the Isle of Arran. The Postbus services operate to and from Brodick Post Office, collecting mail from roadside post-boxes and village post offices along the way. Four or seven seats are available for passengers.

By Car: While cars can be brought onto the Isle of Arran by ferry, it is an extra expense when the road use is so limited. Walkers who 'think green' can be assured that there is no need to take a car to Arran. Bus services on the island are perfectly adequate and reach the starting points of all the walking routes in this guidebook, with the exception of the short road into Glen Rosa. Anyone taking a car to the island should bear in mind that roads are often narrow and winding, with sheep and deer sometimes wandering across them.

Motorists should take care, as deer can be encountered

By Ferry: The only 'internal' ferry service is the little Holy Isle Ferry that runs between Lamlash and Holy Isle. This ferry is subject to seasonal and tidal variations and it is always best to check the sailing schedule in advance, ☎ 01770 600998 or 600349, mobile 079327 86524.

By Helicopter: There is an opportunity to charter a helicopter flight around the Isle of Arran. Arran Heli-Tour flights operate from the Balmichael Visitor Centre, and you can enjoy anything from a simple 10 minute flight to a complete exploratory tour around the island, ☎ 01770 860526 or 860326.

Traveline Scotland: Visitors to the Isle of Arran, or anywhere else in Scotland, can obtain up-to-date information about any kind of public transport from Traveline Scotland. Either ☎ 0870 6082608 or check the website **www.travelinescotland.com**. Services in the region between Arran and Glasgow could also be checked on the SPT website at **www.spt.co.uk**.

Distinctive sandstone milestones stand alongside all the roads around the Isle of Arran

FAMILIARISATION WITH THE ISLE OF ARRAN

Visitors arriving at the ferry terminal at Brodick are confronted by a sign offering only three directions: North, South and West (east is the ferry back to Ardrossan!). There is one main road encircling the Isle of Arran, the A841, which links practically all of the villages on the island. In a clockwise order these include: Brodick, Lamlash, Whiting Bay, Kildonan, Kilmory, Sliddery, Blackwaterfoot, Machrie, Pirnmill, Catacol, Lochranza, Sannox, Corrie and so back to Brodick. There are two roads running across the island. The String, or the B880, runs from Brodick to Blackwaterfoot via Shiskine, with a minor road spur to Machrie. The Ross is a minor road running from Lamlash to Sliddery. All the roads around the Isle of Arran are equipped with distinctive red sandstone milestones. The road system is so simple that it is virtually impossible to get lost, and there are comprehensive bus services along them. Newcomers to the island should consider taking the full-day

15

island tour offered by Stagecoach buses, so that they can see all the villages on the island and take note of the access points for most of the walking routes.

On a few rare occasions the last surviving Clyde paddle steamer, the Waverley, offers visitors the chance to circumnavigate the Isle of Arran. Walkers who plan to complete the Arran Coastal Way might enjoy a cruise around the island to check the nature of the terrain in advance of their trek.

A GEOLOGY CLASSROOM

The Isle of Arran is one of the most varied geological areas in the British Isles. A wag once noted that while some people write to *The Times* when they hear the first cuckoo of spring, others write to the *Arran Banner* newspaper when they hear the chipping of the first geologist of spring! The island is like a huge geological classroom and groups of students will often be seen in careful study.

James Hutton, the redoubtable scientist from Edinburgh, visited the Isle of Arran in August 1787. He was the first person to identify an unconformity; where rocks of widely differing ages rest together at different angles. In fact, an unconformity on the coast north of Lochranza is known to this day as Hutton's Unconformity. Hutton expounded his Theory of the Earth in which mountains were continually being uplifted and

eroded, although few took the great man seriously. Geologists of Hutton's day were divided into the Vulcanists and Neptunists according to whether they believed rocks were formed by volcanic action or by deposition as sediments. Hutton's theory embraced both concepts and today he is widely regarded as the Father of Geology.

The study of the Isle of Arran's geology is very much a specialist subject, but there are a few notes worth bearing in mind. The oldest rocks occur on the northern half of the island. Cambrian strata, originally marine muds and sands, have been altered by tremendous heat and pressure into slates and sparkling schists, often streaked with veins of white quartz. In a semi-circle around this base rock are Devonian strata, composed originally of desert sand dunes, being revealed in an arc from Sannox to Dougarie. A more disjointed arc of Carboniferous strata stretches from Lochranza to Sannox and from Corrie to The String road. These include limestones, sandstones and workable coal measures, all formed in shallow seas or on a swampy delta. Permian strata again indicate desert conditions with sand dunes, and these sandstones take up much of the central and southern parts of the island. Triassic strata stretch across the southernmost part of the island, from Blackwaterfoot to Kildonan, and are composed of muds and sands laid down in a lake or delta system.

Igneous dykes often appear as linear walls of rock, especially along the south coast (Walk 14)

Into this basic layered rock succession were intruded masses of molten rock under great heat and pressure, which had the effect of pushing existing layers into a dome, baking the surrounding strata and altering its mineral structures and appearance. The granite peaks of northern Arran were formed from a massive intrusive 'boss' of granite. Around southern Arran, molten rock was squeezed into bedding planes and joints to create resistant sills and dykes. Some splendid igneous dykes stand out as obvious linear walls of rock, especially around the southern coast, where they are termed 'dyke swarms'.

On a geological time-scale, the final act in the shaping of the Isle of Arran occurred during the Ice Age. The island was prominent enough to support its own ice cap, grinding corries and 'U' shaped valleys quite independent of the massive Highland glaciers scouring out the troughs of the Clyde and Kilbrannan Sound. The power of the ice inexorably grinding into the rocky mountains was one thing, but the weight of the ice was also important. As the Ice Age drew to a close, melt-water raised the sea levels; but as the weight of the ice was lifted from the Earth's crust, there was a corresponding uplift of part of the Earth's surface. This can be noted all around the Isle of Arran, and the Scottish coast, where cobbly raised beaches, marooned sea stacks and marine caves some distance from the sea can be identified.

Walkers with a special interest in geology should use a specific field guide to the geology of the island, such as *Macgregor's Excursion Guide to the Geology of Arran*, edited and revised by J. G. MacDonald and A. Herriot, published by the Geological Society of Glasgow.

A TURBULENT HISTORY

The first hunter-gatherers approaching the Isle of Arran in simple canoes found a forested island with only the highest peaks protruding above the tree canopy. Evidence of this former forest can be seen in some peat bogs, where the trunks, branches and root systems of trees have been preserved. Neolithic hunters and farmers left few discernible traces of their settlements, but they did leave massive chambered burial cairns, most notably around the southern half of the island.

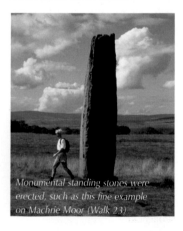

Monumental standing stones were erected, such as this fine example on Machrie Moor (Walk 23)

18

Bronze Age communities left traces of hut circles, stone circles and smaller burial cairns. The best examples are found around Machrie Moor and Blackwaterfoot. The remains point to the development of settled, well-organised communities. The Iron Age is characterised by the construction of small, fortified hill forts, suggesting a measure of insecurity or strife, and again these are to be found mainly around the southern half of the island. The early language forms are unknown, with no written or spoken elements surviving. The Gaelic language of the later Celtic peoples, however, has survived in the Western Isles, although it is not commonly spoken or written on the Isle of Arran today.

St. Ninian is credited with bringing Christianity into Scotland from his base at Whithorn. He and other missionaries sailed around the coastline, visiting small communities and hopping from island to island. Ninian is known to have visited Bute and Sanda, both near Arran, and he died in the year 424. The most notable saint on Arran was St. Molaise, born in the year 566, who lived as a hermit in a cave on Holy Isle and later became the Abbot of Leithglinn in Ireland. He died in the year 639. King's Cave near Blackwaterfoot is thought to have been occupied by early missionaries on inter-island expeditions. The scattered island kingdom was known as Dalriada and was a great Gaelic stronghold.

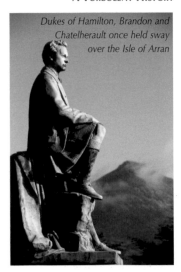

Dukes of Hamilton, Brandon and Chatelherault once held sway over the Isle of Arran

Viking raiding parties hit Iona in the year 759, and later harrassed the Isle of Arran, surrounding islands and coastal areas. Later waves of settlers left traces of farmsteads and Norse placenames; including Goat Fell. The Isle of Arran became, along with neighbouring territories, very much a property of the Norsemen. The great Somerled, originally from Ireland and progenitor of the great clans MacDonald and Ranald, led a force against the Norse in 1156 and became ruler of old Dalriada, although the islands were still nominally under Norse sovereignty.

The emergence of Scotland as an independent state was enhanced following the defeat of the Norse at the Battle of Largs, on the mainland east of the Isle of Arran, in 1263.

The Arran Clearances memorial and a white-washed row of estate cottages at Lamlash (Walk 6)

When Norway sold the islands to Scotland in 1266, Alexander III granted the Isle of Arran to Walter Stewart. Much energy and strife accompanied Robert the Bruce's bitter campaign to secure the Scottish throne, culminating in the Battle of Bannockburn in 1314. For centuries Scottish history was wrought in terms of bitter border disputes with England. The islands, meanwhile, largely continued to exist as Gaelic strongholds with their own clearly defined culture and traditions.

Though little is known of the Isle of Arran's history during certain periods, it is clear that many farmsteads were granted by Scottish kings, who claimed a rent on them. The few stout castles on the island were at some time controlled by the Stewarts before coming into the hands of the Hamiltons. The first Marquis of Hamilton was appointed to administer peace and justice on Arran in

1609, and the Hamilton family is strongly associated with the later development of the island. Successive generations held the title of Dukes of Hamilton, Brandon and Chatelherault, with Brodick Castle as their chief base.

The population of the island increased to the point where many were living in poor 'clachans', or farming settlements, at a time of tremendous social changes. Much has been written about the Arran Clearances of the early 19th century, when people were displaced in favour of sheep, and the population was either re-settled in purpose-built cottages, or forced to emigrate to the New World, most notably Canada. Immediately following the clearances, tourism began to develop and has continued apace, with walking and the enjoyment of the outdoors being a prime pursuit. The Arran Heritage Museum near Brodick offers an insight into the last century of life on the Isle of Arran; a century which has been fairly well documented.

For further details of the Isle of Arran's history, read *Exploring Arran's Past*, by Horace Fairhurst, published by Kilbrannan Publishing.

LAND OWNERSHIP AND ACCESS

Much of the northern half of the Isle of Arran, including many high mountains and bleak, remote wilderness moorland areas, is held by the Arran Estate Trust, Sannox Estate and Strabane Enterprises; they jointly market themselves as Arranland (**www.arranland.net**) and are managed from the Arran Estate Office near Brodick. There is a continuous tall deer fence around the northern half of the island. Within this enclosure, red deer have free range and are prevented from encroaching on neighbouring farms or forestry properties, where they could cause great damage. Deer stalking takes place on the estate from mid-August to mid-October and walkers should be aware of this and take care. Contact the Hillphone on ☎ 01770 302363 in advance of a visit. Culling aims to maintain a healthy deer population of around 600 stags, 700 hinds and 200 calves.

Most of the southern half of the Isle of Arran, and a forest at North Sannox, is owned by the Forestry Commission (**www.forestry.gov.uk**).

The Forestry Commission exists primarily to cultivate rotating stocks of timber. While the forests may seem dark and unattractive to many walkers, there is a policy of allowing virtual free access, except at times when harvesting operations constitute a hazard. Not all the land owned by the Forestry Commission has been planted with trees. The Commission owns almost a fifth of the island, yet has only planted about half that area. There are some very large areas that are unsuitable for planting, including wet moorland and steep hillsides, where good walking and open views can be enjoyed.

The National Trust for Scotland (**www.nts.org.uk**) owns Brodick Castle and its gardens, as well as a sizeable parcel of land which includes, and extends beyond, Glen Rosa, Goat Fell and the surrounding mountains on the island. The land is managed both for conservation and recreation. Walkers are generally free to head in any direction they choose, and this tends to be the busiest mountain area on the island. The proximity of Brodick and the ferry ensures that this will remain the busiest walking area.

The coastal fringe of the Isle of Arran is mostly occupied by small farms and villages. Access to farmland may be quite limited in some areas, and walkers should not cross fields and other enclosures by climbing over walls and fences. Use only regular paths and tracks through farmland, sticking to routes that are already in regular use. There is very good access to the countryside on the Isle of Arran, but it is important that walkers and other visitors respect the rights of landowners and tenants whose livelihood is vested in the land.

ARRAN DEER MANAGEMENT GROUP

The Arran Deer Management Group have placed notices at various access points around northern Arran and these read as follows:

'Walkers are welcome. The members of this Deer Management Group recognise the tradition of free access to the hill. The Deer Management Group is responsible for the management and conservation of the land, in particular the management of red deer. The main deer management aims are:

- to maintain a healthy red deer herd in balance with the natural habitat
- to maintain local employment and through this to support the rural community and local businesses
- to conserve the natural qualities of the land including its wildlife.

The National Trust for Scotland is also a member of this Deer Management Group. Its policies ensure that the public access is unaffected when culling/stalking takes place. Please help the privately owned stalking estates to achieve these aims, particularly during the main stag stalking season from mid-August to mid-October, by:

- avoiding areas where stalking is taking place
- seeking information in advance so that you can plan your visit to avoid disturbance to stalking
- following any local guidance on the day.

All members of this Deer Management Group will be pleased to recommend walking routes which will enable you to enjoy the area.

Information on stalking in Arran is available through the Hillphone answering service, ☎ 01770 302363, whose message is updated daily. Thank you.'

A shortened version of the notice has also appeared in recent years, reading: 'Walkers are welcome to enjoy freedom of access to these hills. This part of Arran has many red deer easily observed while walking.

To maintain a healthy deer population in balance with the natural habitat, control measures are carried out periodically. Mid-August to mid-October is a particularly sensitive time. For up-to-date information on stalking, please call the Hillphone Answer Service on: Brodick 01770 302363.'

SCOTTISH OUTDOOR ACCESS CODE

The *Land Reform (Scotland) Act 2003* has established a statutory right of responsible access to land and inland waters for outdoor recreation. The *Scottish Outdoor Access Code* gives guidance on your responsibilities when exercising access rights. The *act* sets out where and when access rights apply. The *code* defines how access rights should be exercised. The *Scottish Outdoor Access Code* is available on leaflets that can be obtained from Scottish Natural Heritage, tourist information centres and local government offices, as well as on the website **www.outdooraccess-scotland.com**. The following is a summary of the *code*:

Three key principles for responsible access apply to both the public and land managers:

- Respect the interests of other people: be considerate, respect privacy and livelihoods, and the needs of those enjoying the outdoors.
- Care for the Environment: look after the places you visit and enjoy. Care for wildlife and historic sites.
- Take responsibility for your own actions: the outdoors cannot be made risk-free for people exercising access rights; land managers should act with care for people's safety.

The responsibility of recreational countryside users can be summarised as follows:

- Take responsibility for your own actions: The outdoors is a great place to enjoy, but it is also a working environment and has many natural hazards. Make sure you are aware of these and act safely, follow any reasonable advice and respect the needs of other people enjoying or working in the outdoors.
- Respect people's privacy and peace of mind: privacy is important for everyone. Avoid causing alarm to people, especially at night, by keeping a reasonable distance from houses and gardens, or by using paths or tracks.
- Help land managers and others to work safely and effectively: keep a safe distance from any work and watch for signs that tell you dangerous activities are being carried out, such as tree felling or crop spraying. Do not hinder land management operations and follow advice from land managers. Respect requests for reasonable limitations on when and where you can go.

- Care for your environment: follow any reasonable advice or information, take your litter home, treat places with care and leave them as you find them. Don't recklessly disturb or damage wildlife or historic places.
- Keep your dog under proper control: it is very important that it does not worry livestock or alarm others. Don't let it into fields with calves and lambs, and keep it on a short lead when in a field with other animals. Do not allow it to disturb nesting birds. Remove and carefully dispose of dog dirt.
- Take extra care if you are organising an event or running a business and ask the landowner's advice. Check the full version of the *code* for further details about your responsibilities.

ARRAN ACCESS TRUST

The Isle of Arran is a popular destination for walkers, but this can lead to problems of over-use on some paths, or problems with access in other places. The Arran Access Trust seeks to improve the provision of access around the Isle of Arran, repairing damaged and badly eroded paths, even into the highest mountains. The trust has great support on the Isle of Arran and has acquired funding for its work, repairing and restoring several popular footpaths, as well as creating new paths to avoid busy roads. Trust members work with estate managers and farmers, installing gates and stiles at access points around the island. The trust welcomes a wider membership and volunteer workers, who are kept informed of the latest developments around the island. Look out for leaflets produced by the Arran Access Trust, or check their website at **www.arran-access-trust.org.uk**.

Red deer prefer forest cover, but on the Isle of Arran they have adapted to moorland

ISLAND ANIMALS

Arran is an island, so on the way there keep a look out for occasional small whales or dolphins which might be seen from the ferry, and note that seals can be seen basking on rocky and bouldery parts of the shore all around the island. There are no foxes or stoats; there are red squirrels, but no greys. Otters are under pressure from feral mink in the watercourses. Herds of red deer thrive on northern Arran and are selectively stalked and culled as they have no natural predators. Brown hares are often noted around the southern half of the island.

Reptiles are represented by adders, lizards and slow worms, which can all be observed basking in the open on sunny days. There are plenty of frogs in wet places, as well as salmon and trout in the rivers. Dainty dragonflies and butterflies swell the summer air, but the summer months also bring hordes of midges, best defeated by strong sun, a stiff sea breeze, or copious applications of insect repellent!

Seals can often be observed hauled out on boulders, basking contentedly in the sun

A gull's nest found far from the coast on remote moorlands in the middle of the island

Bird life is dominated by golden eagles, hawks and ravens in the mountain environment. Red grouse populate many heathery areas, particularly the southern moorlands. Owls include barn owl, tawny owl, long and short-eared owl. The varied coastal habitats support eider, shag, cormorants, mallard, shelduck, mergansers, redshank, ringed plover, turnstone, oystercatcher, wigeon, goldeneye and many types of gull. Gannets have a colony on Ailsa Craig and may be observed diving spectacularly for fish around the Isle of Arran, while fulmars nest on the cliffs. Herons are found along many watercourses, as well as beside the sea, and there are plenty of forest and meadow species to be spotted. Gulls are not confined to the coast, but may establish breeding colonies on remote moorlands in the centre of the island.

There is a specific field guide to the bird life of the island and keen ornithologists may like to read *Birds of Arran*, by John Rhead and Philip Snow, published by Saker Press.

There is also a periodical called *The Arran Bird Report*, published by the Arran Natural History Society.

ISLAND PLANTS

The plant-life of Arran is another specialist study. The original canopy forest is now reduced to a few ancient stands of oak, ash, rowan or hazel. These areas will often be home to wood sorrel and bluebells. Notable species include the rare Arran service trees, protected from harm in Gleann Diomhan. Forest species include spruce, larch, pines and firs. There are some introduced species that have become nuisances, such as rhododendron and Himalayan balsam. There are also some small, specialised trees to be found in even the most barren mountain areas; generally dwarf willow and creeping juniper, barely lifting themselves above the grass and heather.

The range of habitat types gives a root-hold to some 500 species of flowering plants. A great variety of specialist plants are to be found on the raised beaches and sea cliffs, but there are far too many to list here. Lowland wetlands are often bright with wild iris; slopes may be dominated by invasive bracken; while moorland areas may be flushed purple with heather. Bilberry, bog myrtle and bog asphodel are common on the boggy uplands. The mountain environment supports plants such as alpine lady's mantle, alpine sawwort,

Thrift, or sea pinks, can be found all the way around the rocky coast

starry saxifrage, mossy saxifrage and mountain sorrel.

Some boggy areas feature insectivorous butterwort and sundew. Foxgloves, ragwort and rosebay willowherb are markers of disturbed ground, and hence tend to flourish alongside forest tracks and roads. Tucked away in many dark and damp crevices are an abundance of ferns, for which Arran is notable. Like the coastal plants, ferns are a specialist study.

There is a specific field guide to the flora of Arran which interested botanists may find useful: *Arran's Flora* by Tony Church and Tony Smith, published by the Arran Natural History Society. The *Arran Naturalist* is a periodical also published by the Society.

ACCOMMODATION ON THE ISLE OF ARRAN

There is a wide range of accommodation on the Isle of Arran, but bear in mind that it becomes fully booked at peak periods. Around 5000 people live on the Isle of Arran, but the figure can swell to almost 15,000 in the peak summer period! Either book a bed well in advance, or choose to walk off-season. At the budget level there are a mere handful of campsites around the island, notably: Glen Rosa, near Brodick; Cordon, near Lamlash; Kildonan, in the south-east of the island; Bridgend, near Shiskine; and Lochranza, in the north-west of the island. Wild camping is an option, but refer to the *Scottish Outdoor Access Code* and be scrupulous about making your camps low-key, removing all trace of your stay. There is only one youth hostel on the Isle of Arran, which is at Lochranza, and a well-equipped bunkhouse at Corrie.

The vast bulk of accommodation around the Isle of Arran is self-catering. This can be in the form of apartments, mobile homes, cottages or large houses. Generally, these places offer a full range of facilities, but you should check whether fuel or power is extra, and whether all linen is provided. Standards range from simple to luxurious and are priced accordingly. Self-catering accommodation can be in the villages, or situated in more remote areas.

Food and drink, including Arran specialities, can be found throughout the island (Walk 28)

Bed and breakfast establishments are found all the way around the island, notably in the villages, but also on some of the more remote farms. Small hotels are available at Brodick, Lamlash, Whiting Bay, Kildonan, Lagg, Blackwaterfoot, Catacol, Lochranza, Sannox and Corrie. The largest hotels on the island are near Brodick; the Auchrannie Spa Resort and the Auchrannie House Hotel, with their associated lodges and other facilities.

The Tourist Information Centre at Brodick can offer help and advice about accommodation, and can handle bookings, ☎ 01770 302140 or 302401. There is also an annual holiday and travel guide available that lists accommodation throughout Ayrshire and the Isle of Arran (website **www.ayrshire-arran.com**; email info@ayrshire-arran.com).

FOOD AND DRINK ON THE ISLE OF ARRAN

Despite the fact that much of the Isle of Arran is too bleak, boggy and mountainous to support agriculture, there are rich grasslands around the fringes of the island that support a thriving dairy industry. Few fields are tilled, and are largely given over to livestock. Heavy breeds of cattle include Angus and shorthorn. Hardy little blackface sheep manage on poorer upland grazing, though will be brought into the richer pastures for lambing and fattening. The bleak and

barren northern parts of the island support herds of red deer. Local butchers sell beef, lamb, venison and game and they have their own favourite ways of making pies, puddings and haggis.

The Isle of Arran is self-sufficient in milk, which is of course pasteurised, but not homogenised, so it still has a 'cream-line' and tends to be richer than mass-produced milk. Some of the milk goes towards making a splendid range of cheeses, including the traditional Arran Dunlop, as well as Cheddar, blue, smoked and other flavoured varieties. Cheese manufacture can be observed at Cladach, near Brodick and at the Torrylin Creamery at Kilmory. Goat's cheese is made near Blackwaterfoot. Arran milk is also used to create a local brand of Italian-style ice-creams; refreshing in the summer months and available all around the island.

While the Isle of Arran no longer has a fishing industry, locally caught fish and seafood is available. Creelers smokehouse near Brodick uses local wood and shavings from old whisky barrels to give a distinctive taste to their salmon, kippers and duck. Wild salmon and trout frequent the rivers on the Isle of Arran, but there is also a salmon fishery in Lamlash Bay. In the days when much of the island population lived in poor 'clachans', fare such as salmon and oysters were often regarded as poor man's food!

The Isle of Arran was once famous for potatoes, and old 'lazy beds' or potato ridges can still be seen in depopulated parts of the island where it was once grown as a staple crop. Long after the Arran Clearances, in 1901, a Lamlash man called Donald McKelvie began to breed new varieties of potato, giving them names such as Arran Chief, Arran Cairn, Arran Pilot and Arran Victory. Though many of his varieties are no longer commonly available, a few are still grown on the island, notably at Kingscross near Whiting Bay.

Oats were once a staple crop on the Isle of Arran, contributing to the diet of man and beast, but land is seldom given over to growing cereal crops today. However, Wooleys Bakery at Brodick still produces millions of oatcakes, as well as other fare that serves the needs of islanders and visitors. Two baking ovens, over a century old, handle huge amounts of breads, cakes and biscuits. The bakery is quite close to the Chocolate Shop, where quality chocolates are produced.

Outside Lamlash, Arran Fine Foods once produced only a range of mustards, but has now expanded its range to include chutneys, relishes and fruit preserves. At Cladach, near Brodick, the Arran Brewery produces several types of beer, while at Lochranza the Isle of Arran Distillery produces a range of single malt whiskies and liqueurs.

Visitors to the Isle of Arran could exist quite happily on locally-produced island fare, and such fare is promoted under the banner Taste of Arran. For those who don't know where to start, entire hampers can be made up, either for use on the island, or packaged off-island. Two shops on the Isle of Arran handle a lot of local produce: Taste of Arran at Brodick and the Village Shop at Whiting Bay. Island foodstuffs can be drooled over and ordered through the website **www.taste-of-arran.com**.

Small shops are dotted all the way around the Isle of Arran, and there is a large Co-op supermarket at Brodick. There are many pubs, restaurants and cafés around the island, and many hotels have bars and restaurants that are open to non-residents. Some of the island's golf courses have tearooms attached, and one or two of these offer remarkably extensive menus with plenty of home-made fare. Each of the walking routes in this guidebook indicates whether refreshments are available at the start or finish, or whether you would need to look nearby for food and drink.

THE MAPS

The maps used throughout this guidebook are extracted from the Ordnance Survey Landranger sheet 69. The scale is 1:50,000, which is perfectly adequate for exploring the whole of the Isle of Arran. (Note that the spelling of place names on the OS maps differs from the local spellings which are provided here in the text.) The Ordnance Survey Explorer sheet

361 also covers the Isle of Arran. The scale is 1:25,000, which offers more detail, especially in complex areas such as forests and farmland, or on rocky ridges in the high mountains. The map is printed on both sides of the sheet, with a very generous overlap between the northern and southern halves of the island. Ordnance Survey maps can be obtained widely from bookshops, or ordered through the website **www.ordnancesurvey.co.uk**.

Harvey Map Services produce a two-sided map of the Isle of Arran. One side of the map shows the whole of the island at a scale of 1:40,000, while the other side of the map shows the mountainous northern half of the island at a scale of 1:25,000. There are also small street plans of Brodick, Lamlash and Whiting Bay. Fine attention to detail on this map extends to showing the full extent of boggy ground around the island. Harvey's first mapped the Isle of Arran in 1980 for the arduous Karrimor Mountain Marathon. Harvey's maps are printed on waterproof paper and can be obtained from good bookshops, or ordered through the website **www.harveymaps.co.uk**.

THE WALKS

The walks in this guidebook include a few easy, waymarked forest trails or low-level walks, as well as a dozen or so moderate glen or hill walks. The rest require more effort to complete, heading for the higher mountains and sometimes involving hands-on scrambling. The routes are sometimes along roads or clear forest tracks, sometimes along hill tracks or paths, but may also cross pathless slopes and traverse rocky mountain ridges.

The more off the beaten track the walker wanders, the more care needs to be exercised. Bouldery slopes or tussocky moorlands – places where an ankle is easily turned – are indicated in advance. Steep, rocky scrambles requiring the use of hands are also noted, so cautious walkers can decide whether or not to proceed. All 45 of the walks have been chosen to show off the rich variety of landscape types on the Isle of Arran. They seek both popular and secluded spots, wander along the coast or aim for the heights, taking in wide-ranging views, or searching carefully for some hidden heritage detail.

Longer routes criss-crossing the island can be pieced together using portions of the route descriptions. Many of the walks in this guide overlap, or have sections in common, so that it is easy to extend or shorten many of the routes. By using the excellent bus services around the Isle of Arran, there is no need for walkers to return to their starting point. A few of the walks are linear, and there is plenty of scope for walkers to create longer linear walks simply by linking together adjoining route descriptions.

Holy Isle looks like a mountain marooned at sea when viewed from the Clauchland Hills

TOURIST INFORMATION

The Tourist Information Centre for the Isle of Arran is located at the ferry terminal in Brodick. The office can handle requests about accommodation, attractions, public transport and other services. Beds can be booked in advance, and it is possible to buy specific maps and field guides covering all aspects of the island. Contact: Tourist Information Centre, The Pier, Brodick, Isle of Arran KA27 8AU. ☎ 01770 302140 or 302401, website **www.ayrshire-arran.com**, email info@ayrshire-arran.com.

EMERGENCY SERVICES ON THE ISLE OF ARRAN

The Arran Mountain Rescue Team handles all requests for assistance on the mountains and moorlands around the Isle of Arran. The RNLI operates a lifeboat from Lamlash, though the Isle of Arran is also covered by lifeboats operating from Campbeltown and Largs. There is a hospital at Lamlash, a Health Centre at Brodick and small surgeries around the island. To call for the Police, Ambulance, Fire Service, Mountain Rescue or Coastguard, dial 999 (or the European emergency number 112). Be ready to give full details about the nature of the emergency, and give the operator your telephone number so that they can stay in touch with you if they need further information, or to give you advice and instruction.

Non-urgent matters can be directed to the Police Station at Lamlash, ☎ 01770 302573, or to the hospital at Lamlash, ☎ 01770 600777.

Goat Fell can be seen, and climbed in a
day, from the ferry terminal at Brodick

WALK 1
Goat Fell and Brodick

Distance	17km (10.5 miles)
Height gain	875m/2870ft
Start/finish	Ferry Terminal, Brodick – grid ref. 022359
Terrain	Roads, forest tracks, rugged moorland and a mountain path. The upper parts are steep and stony.
Refreshments	Bars, cafés and restaurants in Brodick. Cafés at the Arran Heritage Centre and Duchess Court. Bar and Arran Brewery at Cladach.

There are walkers who step off the Caledonian MacBrayne ferry at Brodick and straight away head in the direction of Goat Fell, hoping to climb to the summit and return in time to leave the island. It's a grand day out for those who have the energy to complete the ascent between ferries, and this route description is offered just for them.

Others may enjoy Goat Fell by a variety of other routes and tackle the ascent with less urgency. Basically, the route leads along the main road from Brodick, cutting a corner near the Arran Heritage Museum, then starts climbing in earnest above Cladach. The route is a combination of roads, tracks and a well-constructed mountain path. It is quite likely that other walkers will be met on the way there and back as this is the most popular way up and down Goat Fell. The initial road walk could be omitted by catching a bus from the ferry terminal to Cladach, cutting 6km (3.75 miles) from the route. Walkers intending to catch a bus back to the ferry should of course check up-to-date timetables.

Walk away from the **ferry terminal** and turn right to follow the main coastal road through **Brodick**. If any food or drink is needed at the outset, then there are shops along the way where supplies can be obtained. The road runs beside a pleasant green above a rocky shore, then continues between the golf course and **Ormidale Park** on

33

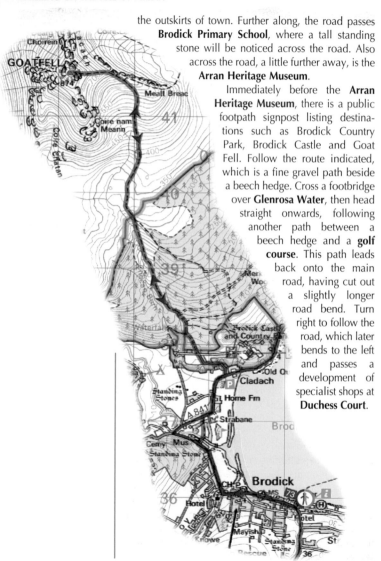

the outskirts of town. Further along, the road passes **Brodick Primary School**, where a tall standing stone will be noticed across the road. Also across the road, a little further away, is the **Arran Heritage Museum**.

Immediately before the **Arran Heritage Museum**, there is a public footpath signpost listing destinations such as Brodick Country Park, Brodick Castle and Goat Fell. Follow the route indicated, which is a fine gravel path beside a beech hedge. Cross a footbridge over **Glenrosa Water**, then head straight onwards, following another path between a beech hedge and a **golf course**. This path leads back onto the main road, having cut out a slightly longer road bend. Turn right to follow the road, which later bends to the left and passes a development of specialist shops at **Duchess Court**.

ARRAN HERITAGE MUSEUM

The Arran Heritage Museum is based in a huddle of whitewashed buildings. Collections of artefacts have been assembled by a voluntary group to illustrate living conditions on the Isle of Arran in the recent past, up to the 1920s. There is a typical cottage, smithy, stable block and numerous agricultural implements. There are displays relating to the island's geology and archaeology, as well as shipping and archive material. Facilities include the Café Rosaburn, while the Rosaburn Lodge Guest House is alongside.

DUCHESS COURT

Duchess Court is a popular attraction for visitors, featuring perfumed products at Arran Aromatics, with the Arran Cheese Company alongside. Both places allow visitors to view their manufacturing processes. There are also gift shops, a café and a seafood restaurant on the site.

After leaving **Duchess Court**, the road bends right to reach **Cladach**, where there is a public footpath sign on the left indicating the start of the climb to Goat Fell. Follow a clear track past the buildings of the **Arran Brewery**. Continue uphill through woods, as signposted 'Goatfell Path'. The slopes are rich in rhododendrons and the track crosses a tarmac driveway that serves nearby **Brodick Castle** (see Walk 2 for details). Just across the driveway there is an information board placed by the National Trust for Scotland.

Follow the track uphill into **Forestry Commission** property. There is a small marker confirming that this is the way towards Goat Fell. As the track climbs, there are waymarked paths leading to left and right at **Cnocan**, but stay always on the clearest track and avoid these other trails. At a higher level, turn left at a **junction** of forest tracks, again indicated as the way to Goat Fell. When a cross-tracks is reached a little further along, go straight through. The path leads through an area where rhodo-dendron scrub has been cut back, passing through a **gateway** in a low drystone wall.

The steep-sided pyramidal peak of Cir Mhòr seen from the summit of Goat Fell

The path climbs through an area where the stands of forest are more distant, and rises on a bracken and heather slope where there are a few scattered stands of birch. The path remains quite clear as it climbs and the surroundings become more rugged. Cross a water channel that has been cut across the hillside then reach a gate in a tall **deer fence**. Beyond the gate the mountain is owned and managed by the National Trust for Scotland.

The path continues uphill at a gentler gradient for a while, and the surface has been restored after suffering years of erosion. There are sections with pitched stone and gravel sufraces, with drains removing excess water, although in some places the path crosses **bare granite** bedrock. The surrounding moorland is mostly wet, grassy, heathery and bouldery. The gradient gradually increases as the path climbs up onto the shoulder of **Meall Breac**. There is a level stance before the path swings more to the left and aims directly for the summit of Goat Fell. This is the toughest part of the ascent, as the path weaves steeply between boulders and granite outcrops.

The summit of **Goat Fell** is reached quite suddenly and is composed of a bare table of granite bearing a few large boulders. There is a trig point at 874m, with a view indicator provided by the Rotary Club of Kilwinning. This is the highest peak on the Isle of Arran. ▶

If a careful check has been made of progress so far, then walkers should be able to gauge whether they are able to catch their intended bus or ferry. The descent needs to be taken carefully at first, but it should take less time than the ascent. It is simply a matter of retracing steps back to the ferry terminal in **Brodick**, or catching a convenient bus on the main road at **Cladach**.

Views are naturally extensive and stretch far into mainland Scotland as well as embracing the Highlands, islands and Northern Ireland.

CLADACH

Brodick village has shifted from the northern side of Brodick Bay to the southern side. Old Brodick is remembered at Cladach, a huddle of old buildings near Brodick Castle. The Old Inn, the Village Inn, a woollen mill and a few houses were all that constituted the village. When the grounds surrounding Brodick Castle were redeveloped in 1853, the woollen mill was moved to Millhouse and the tenants were re-housed at Douglas Place and Alma Terrace. A new school was built in 1854. Tourists had already started visiting the Isle of Arran, frequenting the Old Inn at Cladach, where goat's milk was a speciality! Tourism continued to develop, so that the new village of Brodick became equipped with a new and larger pier, a large hotel, shops and other businesses. Cladach has been redeveloped and retains the the appearance of a small village, with the Arran Brewery being a major attraction. There are also a couple of shops and a bar.

BRODICK

Brodick's main features and facilities can be spotted on the way back to the ferry terminal. In order of appearance they include: Glencloy Road, leading from a beauty salon to the Auchrannie Spa Resort and Glencloy Farm Guest House; Auchrannie Road, leading from a food shop and launderette to the Auchrannie House Hotel; and Knowe Road, leading to the parish church, Hotel Ormidale and Kilmichael Country House.

Arranged along the main road, Brodick Golf Club faces Ormidale Park. The Arran Library and Brodick Hall are beside Brodick Bowling Green, followed by the Brodick Pharmacy, a filling station, Co-op supermarket, Brodick Cycle Hire and a putting green. Across the road are the Post Office, Fire Station and Brodick Bar. Continuing along the main road are the Shanghai Chinese Take-away, Arran Trading Post, Bank of Scotland (with ATM), Inspirations of Arran gift shop and Wooleys bakery.

Several businesses look across the main road to the sea, with ample parking all the way along the road. These include: Stalkers Restaurant, Invercloy Guest House, DIY store, Alexanders gift shop, Arran Estate Agents, Sheepskin Shop, Chocolate Shop, Glenfloral Bed and Breakfast, Isle of Arran Estate Agents, Arran-Asia Trading Company, Book and Card Centre, Royal Bank of Scotland (with ATM), Brodick Health Centre, Dunvegan Guest House and the Shore House Apartments. Next comes Bilslands gift shop and restaurant, crazy golf, Taste of Arran, Arran Craft Gallery, Arran Adventure Centre, Kingsley Mac's Bar, McLaran Hotel and Co-op supermarket.

The McAlpine Hotel incorporates a bar and Italian restaurant, while buildings in the grounds feature an optician, flower shop, Arran Banner newspaper, domestic service centre and barber. The Roman Catholic church is tucked behind. Finally, all in a group at the ferry terminal, are the bus station, a filling station, gift shops and the Tourist Information Centre, ☎ 01770–302140.

WALK 2
Brodick Castle and Country Park

Distance	9km (5.5 miles)
Height gain	300m/985ft
Start/finish	Brodick Castle car park – grid ref. 016380
Terrain	Clear woodland paths and forest tracks, featuring colour-coded waymarks.
Refreshments	There is a café at the car park and a restaurant at Brodick Castle. There is also a bar and the Arran Brewery at Cladach.

The red sandstone towers and turrets of Brodick Castle are easily distinguished, poking above forests on the lower slopes of Goat Fell. Castles have been built and rebuilt on this site for centuries, but the present one dates only from the 19th century and was the seat of the Dukes of Hamilton. Brodick Castle is the centrepiece of the National Trust for Scotland's holdings on the Isle of Arran. It houses silverware and porcelain, paintings and sketches, with rooms full of fine furniture. Wrapped around Brodick Castle is a colourful woodland garden threaded by a variety of paths, lavishly planted with exotic trees and rhododendrons. A separate walled garden has a more regimented layout and features more flowers than trees.

The grounds around Brodick Castle were designated as a Country Park in 1980 and are managed by the National Trust for Scotland and North Ayrshire Council. There are rangers and a Countryside Centre, as well as a series of colour-coded nature trails to explore. The following walk combines three waymarked trails to present a single long walk on the forested hillsides above the castle. Free maps of the trails followed in this walk can be obtained from the shop at the car park, or from the Countryside Centre, or routes can be studied on noticeboards at the start.

Use the main entrance to Brodick Castle and start at the car park beside the shop and café. Bus services run from

the ferry terminal at Brodick all the way into this car park. Information and free trail leaflets are readily available in the shop nearby, and toilets are available. If you want a large, free leaflet map of the trails that are to be followed, obtain one straight away from the shop.

Leave the **car park** and shop by following the road signposted as 'way out', then turn right along a narrow road signposted for the **Countryside Centre**. The centre occupies a huddle of buildings just above the castle and notices explain about the range of nature trails that can be followed. They are: the Duchess's Drive and Merkland Wood Trail with red markers; the Castle Parks Fields and Heronry Pond Trail with blue markers; and the Cnocan Gorge Trail with green markers. All three trails start at the Countryside Centre, heading up a path marked simply as 'trails'.

Follow the colour-coded waymarked path uphill and away from the **Countryside Centre**, crossing a footbridge over a burn. Just to the left is a very short optional loop called **Wilma's Walk**. Wilma's Walk simply heads down through the woods, crosses the burn and ascends gently back to the Countryside Centre.

WILMA'S WALK

A plaque above the Countryside Centre explains: 'Wilma Forgie was Joint Representative at Brodick with her husband John from 1973 until her untimely death in 1983. She was greatly loved by staff and visitors alike and left her mark on Brodick in many ways; one of them was the inspiration for this short walk. It has now been named after her so that those who follow it will remember her.'

The colour-coded waymarked trails are initially signposted for the Hamilton Cemetery and Goat Fell. Follow the path up through a **gate**, across a stile, and uphill again. Rhododendron scrub has been cleared and the woodland floor is light enough to support a riot of grasses and flowers, all vying with each other for attention. Cross a **footbridge**, then climb higher to cross another footbridge. The **Mill Pond** may be observed to the right, but the waymarked route heads to the left and soon begins to run downhill through a clear-felled and replanted forest, featuring views across Brodick Bay. The walled **Hamilton Cemetery** is seen to the left and it can be entered by a fine gateway. Slabs mark the graves of the 11th Duke of Hamilton, Brandon and Chatelherault, as well as the 12th Duke and his wife. Continue along the path until a junction is reached with a clear **forest track**.

Turn right as indicated by **blue and red** waymark arrows, then almost immediately turn left along a track as marked by a **red** waymark arrow. This track is also sign-posted 'Goatfell', rising gently before featuring a slight dip. Another **red** marker points to the right, leading walkers away from the line of the Goat Fell path. The **forest track** rises gently, but offers no really decent views

A remnant ancient woodland fills the Merkland Gorge in Brodick Country Park

at first. A **bench** beside a small burn offers a chance to rest, and there is a fine view over Brodick Bay. The track rises a little more, then swings left, but a **red** marker points straight on along a **grassy track**. The grassy track runs downhill, becoming gravelly before reaching a ford and **footbridge**. There is a turning space for vehicles just beyond.

Another red arrow near the **turning space** points out a path on the right, which descends alongside **Merkland Gorge**. A winding path has been carved into the hillside above the gorge, overlooking a rocky burn full of little waterfalls.

MERKLAND WOOD

Plenty of rhododendron scrub has been cleared in Merkland Wood to help revive what is one of the few ancient woodland sites remaining on the Isle of Arran. With light again able to reach the floor, seedling birch, pine and oak are re-establishing themselves. Sycamore and Douglas Fir are being controlled in accordance with a management plan established by the National Trust for Scotland and the Arran Natural History Society.

Lower down the gorge, turn right to cross a bridge over **Merkland Burn** and follow a forest track almost down to the main coastal road. Off to the left, close to the road, an optional short detour leads to the **Heronry Pool** near Wine Port.

WINE PORT

The rugged bay of Wine Port obtained its name after a French ship ran aground and its cargo of wine and silk was salvaged and taken up to Brodick Castle. The bay has a variety of wildlife habitats, and species that can be spotted include the red-throated diver, black-throated diver, great northern diver, pied wagtail, grey heron, oystercatcher, common sandpiper, red-breasted merganser, eider duck, shelduck and mallard. Grey and common seals can often be observed hauled out on boulders, basking in the sun.

If not making the detour to the **Heronry Pool**, turn right and follow a clear path uphill. This path is waymarked with **blue** arrows, but bear in mind that you should be following them in the opposite direction to the way they are pointing. The path climbs and eventually drifts towards a fence running between **Merkland Wood** and the pastures of the **Castle Parks Fields**. The path turns around the top corner of the fields, then continues up through the woods on a short **flight of steps**.

The path becomes much clearer, bends to the left, runs along a board-walk, then proceeds as an almost level track. Later, follow this gently downhill to cross a little **footbridge**. Keep straight on along the track until a junction is reached which may be recognised as one that was passed earlier in the walk. Turn left and follow a clear **forest track** straight downhill.

When the track bends to the left, take a right turn marked by a **green** arrow indicating the course of the Cnocan Gorge Trail. A broad path climbs uphill and runs across a slope overlooking **Cnocan Burn**. Cross a footbridge and enjoy a view of the **Cnocan Waterfall**. Continue following the path, observing more waterfalls on the way downhill. The **green** waymark arrows lead straight across a tarmac **driveway** serving Brodick Castle, and the path running downstream offers a view of a fine stone arch supporting the driveway. Cross a **footbridge**, which is flanked by flights of steps, then continue along the path which pulls away from the river. The path becomes a well-wooded **track** and rises to a gate. Go through the **gate** and turn right down another **track**. Turn left at the pedestrian entrance to the grounds of Brodick Castle at **Cladach**.

A clear path climbs uphill and after turning right, more of the **green** marker arrows are spotted. The path passes many fine specimens of rhododendrons and some very tall and stately trees. **Brodick Castle** can be seen to the right, but only turn right when you reach the tarmac **driveway** to return to the **car park** where you started. ▶

Walkers who have plenty of time to spare could explore Brodick Castle, or lose themselves on a veritable maze of garden and woodland paths between the castle and the main coastal road.

BRODICK CASTLE

The foundations of Brodick Castle are lost in time. It was garrisoned against Alexander before the Isle of Arran was ceded to Scotland, and there are some rather shaky stories and legends concerning Robert the Bruce and the castle. More solid dates of 1351 and 1406 cover the destruction of the castle by English forces, while Scots themselves attacked the place in 1455. After a rather chequered and battered history, the original features are no longer present as the building has been rebuilt so many times, and the castle has been in the possession of many families. The most notable owners were the Hamiltons, Dukes of Hamilton, Brandon and Chatelherault. The Victorian part of Brodick Castle dates from 1844. In 1853 the castle grounds were redeveloped and tenants in the old village of Cladach were re-housed where the more modern village of Brodick now stands. In an effort to pay death duties, Brodick Castle passed into the care of the National Trust for Scotland in 1957. Some 7000 acres of mountains around Goat Fell and Glen Rosa are also held by the Trust.

Brodick Castle, which also houses a restaurant, is generally open from 1100 to 1630, Good Friday to October. The shop and walled garden are generally open from 1000 to 1630, Good Friday to October, then 1000 to 1530 on winter weekends. To confirm opening times ☎ 01770 302202.

The Country Park is open all year round and Rangers from the Countryside Centre may lead informative guided walks along trails, ☎ 01770 302462.

WALK 3
Brodick and the Clauchland Hills

Distance	10.5km (6.5 miles), with a 1.5km (1 mile) optional extension.
Height gain	290m/950ft
Start/finish	Ferry Terminal, Brodick – grid ref. 022358
Terrain	Good roads, tracks and paths through pastoral and forested countryside.
Refreshments	Plenty of bars, cafés and restaurants in Brodick.

Lying between Brodick and Lamlash, the Clauchland Hills are a low range of hummocky hills under extensive forest cover; a mosaic of mature, clear-felled and replanted areas. A strip of ground of varying width has been left unplanted along the crest of the hills, while the whole of Clauchlands Point remains as tree-free pasture. A stroll over the Clauchland Hills could be accomplished easily from Brodick in a morning or an afternoon. An extension could be made in the direction of Lamlash, but see Walk 5 for a route on that side of the hill.

Walk away from the **ferry terminal** and turn left to follow the main road uphill from **Brodick**, as signposted for Lamlash. The road climbs past a **garden centre**, the Strathwhillan Guest House and the turning for Strathwhillan. Continue uphill and the main road crosses a rise at the Carrick Lodge, then there is a minor road to

45

Goat Fell can be seen from around Corriegills on the way to the Clauchland Hills

the left at **Allandale House**, signposted for Corriegills. This road rises and the scattered settlement of **Corriegills** becomes apparent after reaching a crest on the road. The road runs downhill and passes a number of houses before the tarmac expires at **Corriegills Bridge**. Keep left at a junction of tracks and continue around the hillside, with forest above and pleasant pastoral countryside below. When the track descends towards the **last building**, there is a signposted gravel path off to the right just beforehand.

Follow the path uphill, crossing a little **burn** beside a small water tank. The path crosses a clear-felled and replanted slope in a forest, then continues further up and across the slope, with views only of the sea below and of the rounded hill of **Dun Fionn** ahead. Cross a stile to reach a little gap at the eastern end of the Clauchland Hills, where a fence divides the forest from an area of grass and bracken. Turn right at a **gate and stile** to follow a path into the forest. A sign reads 'Main Road via Clauchland Hills' while the other side of the sign gives directions for Brodick and Lamlash.

The path climbs uphill through the forest along a **grassy ribbon** flanked by bracken. There is a fairly steep pull uphill for a short while, and the trees are generally fairly close to the path. At a higher level the path is more of a roller-coaster, rising more than it falls as it proceeds along the forested crest. There is a more significant **gap** to be crossed before the final pull up to the summit, and although the trees close in on the gap, generally they stand well away from the path and there are later broad strips of heather to either side.

There is a sizable cairn on the summit of the **Clauchland Hills** at 259m. A fine view extends across Brodick Bay to the highest mountains on the Isle of Arran. Unfortunately, due of the height of the trees, there is no corresponding view over Lamlash Bay.

The path leaves the cairn and runs along the **broad ridge** further westwards. Heathery, hummocky hills are crossed and the trend is gradually downhill. The path becomes a little steeper and stonier later, then runs close to the edge of the forest where it may be muddy in places. There are areas of bracken amid the heather, then the path swings left and there is a view across Lamlash Bay after passing a number of **birch trees**. The path reaches a **junction** where a sign reads 'Cairn and Standing Stone'.

Optional extension

Look on the path to the cairn as an optional extension, leading along a forest ride with some squelchy spots to reach **Dunan Mór Cairn**, where a low mound and a partial burial chamber can be inspected.

If the detour is not required, turn right at the **junction** and follow a clear, gravel path straight across a clear-felled and replanted slope. The path crosses a track and leads to the main road linking Brodick and Lamlash at **Cnoc na Dail**, at 114m. The stone circle of this name is off to the right just before reaching the main road, and can be visited by making a short detour.

CNOC NA DAIL

Cnoc na Dail means the 'hill of the meeting place', and is reputed to be the place where crofters would meet regularly in the past to discuss matters of common concern. The word 'dail' has been preserved in modern parlance and is the name given to the Irish Parliament. The Forestry Commission has acquired all the land around Cnoc na Dail, providing facilities such as car parking, picnic tables and waymarked trails.

To continue the walk, cross the road to reach the entrance to a forest car park and **picnic area**. Turn right to follow a path running parallel to the main road in the direction of Brodick. The path leads downhill through a clear-felled and replanted part of **Glenrickard Forest** to reach another small car park and picnic area. A **view indicator** focusses on the highest mountains on the Isle of Arran.

Turn left to follow the path further downhill and keep left as it drifts away from the road and runs down into an area of woodland unaffected by forestry operations. Cross **two footbridges** in the wooded valley, which is known as the **Fairy Glen**. The path runs uphill beside an old drystone wall and becomes broader as it passes through a **gateway**. Walk up through another wooded area and pass a small patch of **heather moorland** around 90m.

A clear track descends past more wooded areas and small fields. Pass a **gate** and continue downhill, walking straight through a cross-tracks to follow a quiet road downhill from the **Glenartney Hotel**. Turn left at a road junction to continue down past the Brodick Bar and Post Office to reach the main coastal road in **Brodick**. Turn right to follow the road back to the **ferry terminal** and walk along a pleasant coastal green. ◀

For a list of facilities along the road through Brodick, see Walk 1

WALK 4
Sheeans and Glen Cloy

Distance	14km (9 miles)
Height gain	550m/1805ft
Start/finish	Cnoc na Dail, between Brodick and Lamlash – grid ref. 018333
Alternative finish	Ferry Terminal, Brodick – grid ref. 022359
Terrain	Good forest paths and tracks, but also pathless moorlands where good navigation is required.
Refreshments	None closer than Brodick and Lamlash

The Sheeans are the Fairy Hills, rising as rounded knolls above Glenrickard Forest. A rather fiddly forest path runs along a series of forest rides towards them, and needs careful route finding. There are no real paths over the exposed moorlands. The route over the Sheeans can be extended around the heads of Gleann Dubh and Glen Ormidale, before a steep descent is made into Glen Cloy, but the whole walk is best attempted in clear weather as the open moorlands could be confusing in mist. A prominent forest path and track are used to bring the circuit to a close. Alternatively, there is a slightly shorter and easier way to finish by heading down through Glen Cloy to reach Brodick, rather than return to Cnoc na Dail.

Start at the **Cnoc na Dail** forest car park and picnic area, at the top of the main road between Brodick and Lamlash. Walk past a **barrier gate** and follow the stony forest track round to the right at a **junction**. Follow the track uphill across a clear-felled and replanted slope, then look carefully on the left to spot a rather **vague path** climbing steeply uphill. Vague though the path is at first, it becomes clearer later. The surface can be grassy, mossy or stony. The path climbs alongside a **small burn** and eventually reaches an intersection of **forest rides**.

Turn right along a grassy, heathery and boggy forest ride, passing a couple of old **wooden posts**. There is a trodden path that can be wet and muddy in places. A **heathery ride** finally exits onto deep heather moorland devoid of paths. Continue uphill on the rugged moorland slope towards the Sheeans. A few **wooden posts** mark the way, then a short, steep climb leads to a trig point on top of the **Sheeans** at 373m. There are views over Brodick and Lamlash Bay, as well as to the mountainous hump of Holy Isle.

Continue walking from the top of the **Sheeans**, across a small, heathery gap, passing a neighbouring summit with a **cairn** at 371m. A broader gap is crossed next, and there is also a **fence** to cross on the next ascent. The aim is to climb uphill on a rugged moorland slope, keeping well back from the awkward cliffs of **Creag nam Fitheach**. Westwards lie seemingly endless rugged moorlands, where the walking can be quite difficult, especially in mist.

The best strategy is to try contouring the moorland slopes, heading roughly northwards at approximately 370–380m around the head of **Gleann Dubh**. There are a few small streams to be crossed, as well as a strange area blanketed in scrubby growths of willow.

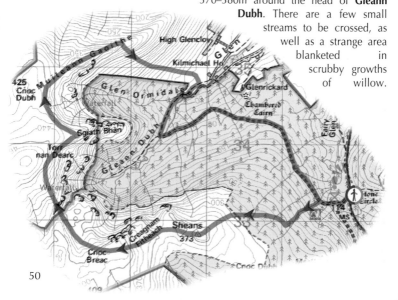

The heathery hump of Sgiath Bhan rises above the forested head of Glen Cloy

There is the chance to pick up occasional sheep paths, which can be linked to provide a route towards the heathery prow of **Sgiath Bhan** at 427m. There is a small cairn in an area of boulders, and a vague path swings round the moorland slope behind the hump of Sgiath Bhan.

Contour around the moorland slopes at the head of **Glen Ormidale**, continuing across a broad gap between Cnoc Dubh and Muileann Gaoithe. There are two little summits on **Muileann Gaoithe**, the first with a small cairn at 401m and the second without. There is now a clear path along the sharply defined ridge of Muileann Gaoithe, which can be followed down to the corner of a **fence**. Turn right away from the fence to descend into **Glen Cloy**. A steep slope of heather and bracken gives way to a gentler slope of tussocky grass. Walk down to a **forest fence** and continue downhill alongside it. Rampant growths of bog myrtle are passed. Turn left to follow another fence at the foot of the slope and go through a **gate** into a field.

51

WALKING ON THE ISLE OF ARRAN

Turn right to walk diagonally through the field, back towards the **Glenrickard Forest**, reaching a sign at a gate where a path enters the forest. The sign indicates that this is the way back to Cnoc na Dail. There are views back around the head of the glen to Sheeans and Sgiath Bhan. The path reaches a broad track and a bridge in **Gleann Dubh**. Follow the track across the bridge, rising gently at first, then more steeply later. At a higher level, the track gradient eases, and there are good views back to the highest peaks of Arran. The track finally leads down to the car park and picnic area beside the main road at **Cnoc na Dail**.

Alternative finish

Instead of turning right on the descent to approach **Glenrickard Forest**, a left turn offers an easy route through **Glen Cloy** to finish at Brodick. Simply pick up a path that leads to a farm where there is stabling for horses. A **riverside track** runs away from the farm, but when it turns left, keep walking straight ahead, following a wooded **path** close to the river. This can be muddy and stony in places, but is clear and obvious. It passes a small development of **lodges** and an access road runs past the entrance to the **Auchrannie House Hotel**. Continue along Auchrannie Road to pass an Army Cadet base, a garage and gallery, launderette and food shop. Turn right to follow the main coastal road through **Brodick** to finish at the **ferry terminal**. ◀

For a list of facilities along the road through Brodick, see Walk 1.

WALK 5
Lamlash and the Clauchland Hills

Distance	10km (6 miles)
Height gain	280m/920ft
Start/finish	Marine House Hotel, Lamlash – grid ref. 033316
Terrain	Easy roads, tracks and paths through forest, over hills and along the coast.
Refreshments	Bars, cafés and restaurants in Lamlash.

The Clauchland Hills are a low range of hills between Lamlash and Brodick. Although they are largely under forest cover, a broad strip has been left unplanted along the crest of the range, and the land extending to Clauchlands Point remains a pleasant pastoral landscape. A circular walk based on Lamlash takes in the Clauchland Hills, Clauchlands Point and the stretch of coastline leading back to Lamlash. Holy Isle is seen at close quarters and appears like a mountain marooned at sea. There is the option on this walk to make a detour and visit ancient stone remains. Other forest paths and tracks could be used to extend the route. See Walk 3 for details of another walk over the Clauchland Hills offering links with Brodick.

Start from **Lamlash** and leave the village by following the main road for Brodick, uphill from the **Marine House Hotel**. An old milestone might be noticed on the left just after passing the mobile homes on Park Avenue. **Lamlash Golf Club** is on the right just at the top edge of the town. The pavement runs out shortly afterwards, but a **path** has been provided between the road and an adjacent field. Look back to see Holy Isle completely filling Lamlash Bay.

Later, the path crosses a **footbridge** and passes into a clear-felled and replanted forest. It drifts away from the road as it climbs further into **Glenrickard Forest**, and reaches a small car park and picnic area. Cross the

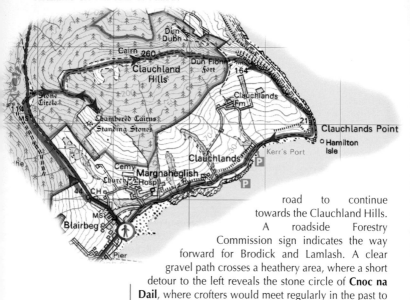

road to continue towards the Clauchland Hills. A roadside Forestry Commission sign indicates the way forward for Brodick and Lamlash. A clear gravel path crosses a heathery area, where a short detour to the left reveals the stone circle of **Cnoc na Dail**, where crofters would meet regularly in the past to discuss matters of common concern.

The clear path runs through a clear-felled and replanted forest. It crosses a **forest track** and is firm and dry as it runs uphill, featuring views across Lamlash Bay. Later, there is a sign pointing in two directions at a **junction**. The path to the left is marked as 'Forest Walk', while a path to the right is marked 'Cairn and Standing Stone'.

Optional extension

Look on the path to the cairn as an optional extension, leading along a forest ride with some squelchy spots to reach **Dunan Mór Cairn**, where a low mound and partial burial chamber can be inspected.

If this detour is not required, turn left and walk uphill along a wide unforested strip onto the Clauchland Hills. The path climbs uphill and swings to the right after passing a number of **birch trees**. The path runs close to the edge of the forest for a short while and can be muddy

*Looking back towards the village of Lamlash,
with Holy Isle rising from the bay*

in places. After climbing the steep and stony path for a while, the path rises more gradually across heathery, hummocky terrain. The summit of the **Clauchland Hills** bears a large cairn at 259m. There is a good view across Brodick Bay to the highest mountains on the island. Unfortunately, because of the height of the trees, there is no corresponding view over Lamlash Bay.

There is a significant **gap** in the Clauchland Hills just beyond the summit, where the heathery swathes either side of the path become narrower and trees close in on the path. As the path proceeds along a roller-coaster course, the trend is gradually downhill and the ground alongside is covered in grass and bracken. There is a steeper run downhill to the edge of the forest, where a sign stands beside a **gate and stile**. The sign points left to Brodick and right to Lamlash, but the direction to take is straight ahead, crossing the stile to follow a grassy path onto a domed summit crowned by a trig point at 164m. This is **Dun Fionn**, the site of an Iron Age hill fort. Views across Lamlash Bay include the dramatic hump of Holy Isle. Note also the scrubby raised beach closer to hand near **Corriegills Point**.

The grassy path runs beyond the domed summit and proceeds down a slope of bracken close to a **cliff edge**. Various devices have been employed to protect farm stock from the cliffs. The remains of an earthen embankment, a drystone wall and at least two fences have all been constructed along the cliff line. Go through a **gate** into a field and proceed to the end of **Clauchlands Point**. There is a rocky protuberance offshore, **Hamilton Isle**, which is often used as a perch by gulls, cormorants and shags. A small quarry has been cut into the end of the point, and a **clear track** can be followed away from it. The track hugs the shore, passing a couple of concrete lookout posts, eventually joining a **minor road** at a corner. This road also hugs the shore and has a few small parking spaces along its length.

Public footpath signposts at **Margnaheglish** point back to Clauchlands Point, as well as uphill to Dun Fionn. The shore road is lined with houses and other notable build-

Holy Isle is seen from the bouldery shore on the way back to the village of Lamlash

ings. The HF Holidays base is passed at **Altachorvie**, on a bend in the road, and later you pass The Shore bed and breakfast, a **disused church** and the Council Offices. The road reaches the **Marine House Hotel**, where a left turn leads into the village of **Lamlash**. ▶

See Walk 6 for a list of facilities in the village

LAMLASH

While Brodick may appear to be the capital of the Isle of Arran to casual visitors, Lamlash is actually the administrative centre, containing the high school, hospital and police station for the island. The name Lamlash is derived from St. Molaise, who lived as a hermit on Holy Isle before becoming the Abbot of Leithglinn in Ireland. Holy Isle was previously known as Eilean Molaise. As the island offers good shelter to Lamlash Bay, the place has been used on occasions to shelter entire fleets of ships. King Hakon of Norway assembled his fleet in the bay before his disastrous performance at the Battle of Largs in 1263. During the Great War, parts of the North Atlantic and Home Fleets also weighed anchor here.

Lamlash in its present form dates only from around 1830. Families had been cleared from old clachans and new buildings were constructed to house them. The parish church dates from 1884 and was built by the 12th Duke of Hamilton. The hospital was constructed partly as a war memorial and opened in 1922. The high school was completed in 1939, but did not take its first pupils until 1946.

WALK 6
Sheeans and The Ross

Distance	14km (8.5 miles)
Height gain	440m/1445ft
Start/finish	Marine House Hotel, Lamlash – grid ref. 033316
Terrain	Roads, forest tracks and paths at first, but also rugged, pathless moorlands.
Refreshments	Bars, cafés and restaurants in Lamlash.

The Sheeans, also known as the Fairy Hills, are usually climbed using a forest path from Cnoc na Dail, as detailed in Walk 4, where the route crosses the Sheeans and traverses rugged moorlands around the head of Gleann Dubh and Glen Ormidale. This route from Lamlash, however, crosses the Sheeans on a rugged moorland walk around the head of Benlister Glen. While this is a good option to consider when cloud blankets the higher mountains, it is not particularly recommended as an excursion in its own right in mist. The rough, exposed, barren, pathless moorlands require competent navigation. Much of the route is on moorland slopes, rather than on clearly defined ridges and summits. Buses could be used to reach Cnoc na Dail from Lamlash, shortening the route a little.

Start from **Lamlash** and leave the village by following the main road for Brodick, uphill from the **Marine House Hotel**. An old milestone might be noticed on the left just after passing the mobile homes on Park Avenue. **Lamlash Golf Club** is on the right just at the top edge of the town. The pavement runs out shortly afterwards, but a **path** has been provided between the road and an adjacent field. Look back to see Holy Isle completely filling Lamlash Bay.

Later, the path crosses a **footbridge** and passes into a clear-felled and replanted forest. It drifts away from the road as it climbs further into **Glenrickard Forest**,

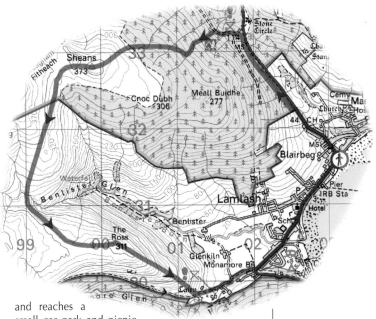

and reaches a small car park and picnic area. Turn left to walk up past a **barrier gate** and follow the stony forest track round to the right at a **junction**. Follow the track uphill across a clear-felled and replanted slope, then look carefully on the left to spot a rather **vague path** climbing steeply uphill. Vague though the path is at first, it becomes clearer later. The surface can be grassy, mossy or stony. The path climbs alongside a **small burn** and eventually reaches an intersection of **forest rides**.

Turn right along a grassy, heathery and boggy forest ride, passing a couple of old **wooden posts**. There is a trodden path that can be wet and muddy in places. A **heathery ride** finally exits onto deep heather moorland devoid of paths. Continue uphill on the rugged moorland slope towards the Sheeans. A few **wooden posts** mark the way, then a short, steep climb leads to a trig point on top of the **Sheeans** at 373m. ▶

There are views over Brodick and Lamlash Bay, as well as to the mountainous hump of Holy Isle.

Trig point on the summit of the Sheeans, where there are views towards northern Arran

Westwards are empty moorlands and the dome of Beinn Bhreac, while northwards, beyond the Sheeans, are the jagged peaks of northern Arran stretching from Beinn Nuis to Goat Fell.

Continue walking from the top of the **Sheeans**, across a small, heathery gap, passing a neighbouring summit with a **cairn** at 371m. A broader gap is crossed next, and there is also a **fence** to cross on the next ascent. Aim to climb gradually uphill on the rugged, **pathless moorland** slope, but also drift well to the left at the same time. There is no need to climb all the way to the crest of the moorland, but be content simply to pick a way across the slope in a roughly southerly direction, contouring for a while above 350m. There are areas of tough heather, tussocky grass and boggy patches. The route descends into a hollow in the moorland and crosses a **small burn**, just before it breaks into a series of **waterfalls** at the head of **Benlister Glen**.

Once across the burn, climb straight up the heathery slope, still heading southwards, but then swing to the left to gain a broad grass and heather crest. Head eastwards, towards **The Ross**, which seems to stand directly in front of the shape of Holy Isle. The broad crest can be boggy in places, and there are some very vague paths. A short ascent on heather leads to a small **summit cairn** in a patch of short grass at 311m. Enjoy the views one last time. Holy Isle is well displayed in Lamlash Bay, with the broad shoulders of Tighvein filling the southern prospect. ◄

The descent starts with a walk along the heathery crest of **The Ross**, passing another small cairn. Continue downhill more steeply, crossing heather and grass, then bracken on the lower slopes. There is a vaguely trodden path leading down to the road, but it is easily lost in the bracken towards the end. As there are also gorse bushes on the lower slopes, extra care is needed. Aim just to the right of a **house** seen at the foot of the slope. Once **The Ross road** has been reached, turn left to follow it across a cattle grid, passing the entrance to the forest walks at **Dyemill**, continuing past the **Arran Fine Foods** factory to reach a bend on the main road.

Turn left along the main road. If a bus comes along the road, then use it to return through **Lamlash**. If not, then walk along the road and, later, along the grassy strip between the road and the shore, to return to the **Marine House Hotel**, or any other point where you wish to finish.

LAMLASH

Practically all the shops and businesses in Lamlash are passed on the walk from the Arran Fine Foods factory to the Marine House Hotel. Facilities from south to north include: Arran Fine Foods, Middleton Caravan and Camping Park and a couple of bed and breakfast establishments.

Next come the Arran high school, police station, butcher/grocer, medical centre, coastguard, tennis courts and putting green, and a picnic area on the coastal green. After the parish church comes the Co-op store, Aldersyde Hotel, Ship House (a shop) and the Lamlash Garage. Lamlash Post Office is located at the end of a terrace of estate cottages, with a memorial to the Arran Clearances on a green in front of the cottages.

After that is the Glenisle Hotel, Lilybank bed and breakfast, Redhouse Pharmacy and the Made in Arran crafts and tearoom. Clustered around the pier are the Pierhead Tavern, play area, toilets, Old Pier Tearoom, Johnston's Marine Stores, Lifeboat Station, Arran Yacht Club and Holy Isle Ferry. A couple of shops and galleries are followed by the Lamlash Bowling Club and the Drift Inn. The Marine House Hotel stands at a road junction, where a right turn leads to the council offices, a disused church, The Shore Bed and Breakfast, hospital and the HF Holidays base at Altachorvie.

WALK 7
Lamlash to Brodick

Distance	6km (3.75 miles)
Height gain	115m/375ft
Start	Marine House Hotel, Lamlash – grid ref. 033316
Finish	Ferry Terminal, Brodick – grid ref. 022359
Terrain	Easy forest paths and country tracks.
Refreshments	Plenty of bars, cafés and restaurants in Lamlash and Brodick.

One of the busiest roads on the Isle of Arran is the one running between Brodick and Lamlash, crossing a forested gap in the Clauchland Hills at Cnoc na Dail. This was never a road that could be recommended for walking, but good paths have recently been created running parallel to the road, and these can be linked with an old path running through the Fairy Glen. An easy and pleasant walk can be enjoyed from Lamlash to Brodick, or vice-versa, keeping safely away from the traffic. Clear-felling in Glenrickard Forest has opened up fine views of the northern mountains of Arran, while the original woodland cover in the Fairy Glen has been spared the forester's axe.

Start from **Lamlash**, and if you need anything before starting, a list of the main facilities in the village can be found in Walk 6. Leave the village by following the main road for Brodick, uphill from the **Marine House Hotel**. An old milestone might be noticed on the left just after passing the mobile homes on Park Avenue. **Lamlash Golf Club** is on the right just at the top edge of the town. The pavement runs out shortly afterwards, but a **path** has been provided between the road and an adjacent field. Look back to see Holy Isle completely filling Lamlash Bay. Later, the path crosses a **footbridge** and passes into a clear-felled and replanted forest. It drifts away from the road as it climbs further into **Glenrickard Forest**, and reaches a small car park and picnic area.

It is worth crossing the main road, following a path for a few paces, then turning left to see a stone circle at 114m at **Cnoc na Dail**. The name means 'hill of the meeting place', and is reputedly where crofters would meet regularly in the past to discuss matters of common concern. Come back across the road to continue the walk.

Follow a path running parallel to the main road in the direction of Brodick. The path leads downhill through a clear-felled and replanted part of **Glenrickard Forest** to reach another small car park and picnic area. A **view indicator** focusses on the highest mountains on the Isle of Arran. Turn left to follow the path further downhill and keep left as it drifts away from the road and runs down into an area of woodland unaffected by forestry operations.

Cross **two footbridges** in the wooded valley, which is known as the **Fairy Glen**. The path runs uphill beside an old drystone wall and becomes broader as it passes through a **gateway**. Walk up through another wooded area and pass a small patch of **heather moorland** around 90m.

A clear track descends past more wooded areas and small fields. Pass a **gate** and continue downhill, walking straight through a cross-tracks to follow a quiet road downhill from the **Glenartney Hotel**. Turn left at a road junction to continue down past the Brodick Bar and Post Office to reach the main coastal road in **Brodick**. Turn right to follow the road back to the **ferry terminal**, and walk along a pleasant coastal green. ▶

For a list of facilities along the road through Brodick, see Walk 1.

WALK 8
Holy Isle from Lamlash

Distance	7km (4.5 miles)
Height gain	345m/1130ft
Start/finish	North Jetty, Holy Isle – grid ref. 053309
Terrain	A rugged hill walk on a clear path, followed by a clear, level, easy coastal walk. To check Holy Isle Ferry schedules, ☎ 01770 600998 or 600349, mobile 079327 86524.
Refreshments	Tea and coffee from the Boathouse on Holy Isle. Bars, cafés and restaurants in Lamlash.

Holy Isle was bought by a community of Buddhists and has been designated as a Sacred Site. The community is happy to allow access to the island, which had occasionally been closed to visitors by previous owners. However, visitors should respect the wishes of the community, who ask only that the island is respected. Smoking, alcohol, drugs, pets and sound systems are not permitted, and there is no access to the eastern part of the island, which is maintained as a nature reserve and refuge for rare animal breeds.

The visit starts with a ferry from Lamlash to a jetty at the northern end of the island. The route rises along the crest of the island, visiting its summit at Mullach Mòr, then descends southwards. The return northwards is along a clear, level coastal path, brightened with interesting and intricate rock paintings, taking in a cave inhabited for 20 years by St. Molaise.

The ferry from **Lamlash** to Holy Isle moors at a short jetty near the **Centre for World Peace and Health** at the northern end of the island. On stepping ashore, a plaque displays a map of the island and one of the island residents may well meet the ferry and welcome visitors ashore. If walkers need any specific information about Holy Isle, this would be a good time to ask, though there are also leaflets available at the nearby **Boathouse**.

THE HOLY ISLE FERRY

The Holy Isle Ferry generally operates on a daily basis from May to September, running hourly between Lamlash Old Pier to Holy Isle. The first trip from Lamlash is generally 1000 and the final departure from Holy Isle is generally 1700. The crossing time is only around 10 minutes, but is quite expensive. Sailings are subject to demand, the weather and tidal conditions. Spring and autumn services run at a reduced level, while winter services need to be arranged with the ferryman. It is wise to check sailings in advance, ☎ 01770 600349 or 600990. Tours and fishing trips are also available.

There is a path rising through the field to the left of the centre, simply signposted 'to the top'. It continues rising beyond a **stile** at a gap in a drystone wall, crossing bracken and heather where thousands of young trees have been planted. The path swings to the right and is marked by posts bearing arrows. Cross a **stile** over a fence and continue climbing uphill through more deep heather. The high mountains of northern Arran begin to rise above the low, forested rise of the Clauchland Hills. On a higher shoulder, Whiting Bay and the pyramidal island of Ailsa Craig appear in view. The path is narrow, but clearly marked and trodden. It rises more steeply up a slope of heather, wrinkled boulders and outcrops of rock. The top of **Mullach Beag** (246m) bears a cairn and offers fine views around both Lamlash and Whiting Bay, while ahead the taller Mullach Mòr beckons.

There is a short descent in two stages to a **gap** in the middle of Holy Isle. While a path

65

The Centre for World Peace and Health, where the walk on Holy Isle commences

may be noted sneaking off to the right, there is another path making a direct ascent of Mullach Mòr. This stony path reaches rocky places where hands will be required for balance, though there are plenty of good holds. An easier stretch of path continues to the highest point on the island, **Mullach Mòr**, where a trig point on stands at 314m (it may have prayer flags around it). The summit ridge is fairly narrow and composed of grass, heather, bilberry and rocky outcrops. ◀

The path runs roughly southwards, descending more and more steeply on **Creag Liath**. There is one stretch where it picks its way down a slope of worn, broken rock. On a gentler shoulder, beware of dark, deep, **narrow fissures** in the rock. Stick strictly to the path as indicated by ropes. Note the **cabin** on the hillside to the right, which is inhabited by the Venerable Lama Yeshe Losal Rinpoche. The path descends one more rounded, heathery ridge, joining a clearer path in an area of bracken. Turn left at this point if you wish to visit the square **Pillar Rock Lighthouse**, though there is no further access beyond. Turn right to walk towards another lighthouse and the former lighthouse keeper's cottages, now a long-term **retreat centre**, with no

Views take in most of Holy Isle, the forests and moorlands of southern Arran and the high mountains of northern Arran. A good stretch of the Clyde is also in view, along with Ailsa Craig.

Rock paintings in traditional Tibetan styles are seen on the west coast of Holy Isle

access to visitors. The lighthouse buildings face Kingscross Point, which is the closest point on the Isle of Arran to Holy Isle.

Stay on a **grassy path**, as directed, leading through the bracken, running roughly northwards from the lighthouse. The path is obvious, but is also marked by poles carrying electricity lines. While following the path, keep an eye open to the right, to spot a number of splendid **rock paintings**. These were created by an artist called Dekyi Wangmo, who was working to a series of traditional Tibetan designs. The path is slightly more rugged as it turns around a bay fringed with a few trees. Look out for steps to the right, rising to **St. Molaise's Cave** at the base of a cliff.

ST. MOLAISE

The most notable saint on Arran was St. Molaise, born in the year 566. He lived as a hermit in this cave on Holy Isle for 20 years. His Judgement Seat and Healing Spring are nearby, and a ladle is provided for those who wish to taste the water. Molaise became the Abbot of Leithglinn in Ireland and died in the year 639. Holy Isle was previously known as Eilean Molaise.

The path is smooth and level as it turns round the shingly **White Point**. It is surfaced in short grass and runs through an area of bracken that has been planted with young trees. The **Centre for World Peace and Health** at the northern end of the island is reached and the walk is brought to a close. Tea and coffee may be available at the **Boathouse** while you wait for the ferry, or you could explore the intriguing **Mandala Garden**. There is abundant information about the Holy Island Project to take away. Donations to assist in the work being carried out on the island may also be made.

HOLY ISLAND PROJECT

Residents of Holy Isle include Tibetan Buddhist monks, nuns and lay people, as well as people of other faiths and volunteers helping with conservation or construction work. As the island has been designated as a Sacred Site, residents observe five Golden Rules:

- to protect all life and refrain from killing
- to respect other's property and refrain from stealing
- to speak truthfully and refrain from lying
- to encourage health and refrain from all intoxicants
- to respect others and refrain from sexual misconduct.

The northern end of the island is where the Centre for World Peace and Health is located. Accommodation and full vegetarian board are available to visitors, and a variety of courses are offered. The Boathouse generally offers tea and coffee, as well as a few gifts and information. The southern end of the island houses a long-term Buddhist retreat centre. Traditionally, retreats last for three years and three months, and visitors should cause no disturbance near the buildings. A conservation project involves bracken control, tree planting and the development of a nature reserve on the eastern side of the island. Rare animal breeds may also be spotted. For more information, ☎ 01770 601100, or visit the website **www.holyisland.org**.

WALK 9
Tighvein and Monamore Glen

Distance	10km (6 miles)
Height gain	450m/1475ft
Start/finish	Dyemill car park, near Lamlash – grid ref. 015297
Terrain	Forest tracks and paths are clear, but there are also rugged, pathless moorlands, requiring careful navigation.
Refreshments	None closer than Lamlash.

All walks on the flanks of Tighvein are rough and tough as there are no trodden paths across the hill. There is, however, a waymarked forest trail which runs from the Dyemill car park near Lamlash to the lonely moorland pool of Urie Loch. The loch is only a short walk from the summit of Tighvein, so the waymarked trail offers the easiest approach. Finding a way off the summit of Tighvein is reserved for those who can navigate competently across featureless moorlands, especially in mist. There is a route roughly northwards across Cnoc Dubh and Garbh Bheinn that allows a descent to the head of Monamore Glen without grappling with forest plantations.

This walk starts at the Dyemill car park on The Ross road outside Lamlash. The road is signposted for 'Sliddery via Ross' off the main road south of Lamlash, and is used by occasional Post Bus services. The turning looks as though it is the entrance to the Arran Fine Foods factory, as the factory buildings stand on both sides of the road. The road runs up past the Dyemill Lodges, then reaches a forest track on the left. A sign beside the road reads 'Forestry Commission. Dyemill. Car park and picnic area with forest walks to Lagaville, Urie Loch, Whiting Bay and Kilmory.' There is a grassy area with picnic tables to the right of the forest track, with car parking available beside Monamore Burn.

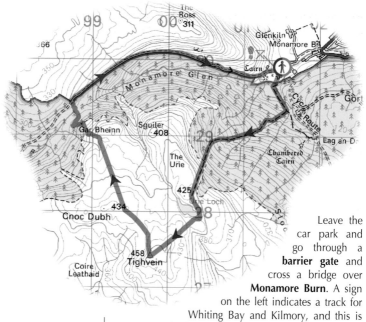

Leave the car park and go through a **barrier gate** and cross a bridge over **Monamore Burn**. A sign on the left indicates a track for Whiting Bay and Kilmory, and this is marked as suitable for cyclists. A sign to the right indicates the 'Lagaville Walks' and the hill walk to Urie Loch. Follow the **riverside path** a short way upstream alongside Monamore Burn, then cross a **footbridge** on the right over a smaller burn. Turn left and walk upstream, passing oak, birch and other trees alongside the burn, which contrast with the clear-felled and replanted forest alongside. Climb up a few **steps** and walk alongside a wooden fence. A footbridge on the left overlooks a small waterfall in a **rocky gorge**. Don't cross the footbridge, which offers only a rapid return to the Dyemill car park.

A red arrow beside the **footbridge** points uphill for Urie Loch and care is needed in wet weather as exposed tree roots could be slippery. After passing the next **red marker** the path climbing uphill is stonier underfoot. The path pulls away from the burn on a clear-felled and replanted slope. It briefly returns to the **burn** and then enters a higher part of the forest. The path running uphill is muddy in places and is flanked with heather and later with bracken as it climbs. There is a gentler stretch, then a steeper climb. The path climbs up a **forest ride**, which is mostly grassy, then climbs up a steep slope of coarse grass. It cuts diagonally left across a heathery slope studded with a few boulders, running along the top edge of the forest beneath the rugged slopes of **Creag na h' Ennie**.

A final red marker post at the top corner of the forest points across a rise of squelchy moorland over 400m. The path passes a couple of boulders and then runs down to the shores of **Urie Loch**. This is the end of the waymarked trail and anyone whose navigation is not up to scratch should consider retracing steps to the Dyemill car park. Those who can navigate confidently across bleak and **pathless moorlands** can continue and complete a rough, tough moorland and forest circuit. Walk south-west from the head of Urie Loch. There is no trodden path over the heather, and the summit of **Tighvein** is not seen until at close quarters, but bears both a cairn and trig point at 458m. Views of the immediate surroundings embrace rugged, rolling moorlands. Northwards the higher mountains of the Isle of Arran are well displayed.

Dark and foreboding at times, sprawling moorlands surround Tighvein's summit

Leaving the summit of **Tighvein**, there is only a short, steep slope before more gentle gradients lead roughly north-west towards the broad moorland rise of **Cnoc Dubh**. The heather cover is broken only by a couple of grassy areas, with even fewer small boulders poking through, and many channels of squelchy sphagnum moss. Side-step the channels where possible, but keep the ultimate objective of Gar Bheinn in line, lying more to the north. The prow of **Gar Bheinn** is where the moorland slope gives way to forest plantations at the head of Monamore Glen. Look carefully down the steep, heather slope to spot wheel marks left by quad bikes. These reveal a gap through the trees, where a **forest ride** can be accessed. Turn right along the ride, cutting across the slope, then turn left, walking down along another ride to cross a broad and boggy ride. A wet and boggy path heads uphill along a narrower ride, reaching the top of **The Ross road**.

Turn right to follow The Ross road across a **cattle grid**, then gradually downhill. There is forest on the right to the right practically all the way, but up to the left is a steep slope culminating at **The Ross**. At the bottom of the road, there is a turning on the right where a forest road leads straight back to the **Dyemill** car park where the walk started. Post Bus services only run *up* the road, never *down* it, so they are no use at the end of this walk.

ARRAN FINE FOODS

There was once a water-powered meal mill at the foot of Monamore Glen. It was closed in 1967, and being unsafe, it was demolished. The Arran Fine Foods factory occupies the same site as the old mill, and originally manufactured a range of quality mustard products. The factory now produces a range of fine jams, chutneys and other preserves. Samples can be bought from the factory shop adjoining the visitor's car park.

WALK 10
Tighvein and Urie Loch

Distance	12km (7.5 miles)
Height gain	530m/1740ft
Start	Dyemill car park, near Lamlash – grid ref. 015297
Terrain	Forest tracks and paths are fairly clear, but there are also rugged, pathless moorlands to negotiate, requiring careful navigation.
Refreshments	None closer than Lamlash.

The highest point in southern Arran is the broad, bleak, heather moorland of Tighvein. All walks on its flanks are rough and tough as there are no trodden paths across the hill. There is, however, a waymarked forest trail which runs from the Dyemill car park near Lamlash to the lonely moorland pool of Urie Loch. The loch is only a short walk from the summit of Tighvein, so the waymarked trail offers the easiest approach. Walkers who enjoy crossing empty moorlands can extend this walk beyond the summit of Tighvein. Care is needed with route finding, and easy descents from the moorland are limited. Forest almost completely encircles Tighvein, and there are few decent ways down to the tracks that are hidden deep inside the forest. Forest tracks and other waymarked trails are linked to provide a route back to the Dyemill.

This walk starts at the Dyemill car park on The Ross road outside Lamlash. The road is signposted for 'Sliddery via Ross' off the main road south of Lamlash, and is used by occasional Post Bus services. The turning looks as though it is the entrance to the Arran Fine Foods factory, as the factory buildings stand on both sides of the road. The road runs up past the Dyemill Lodges, then reaches a forest track on the left. A sign beside the road reads 'Forestry Commission. Dyemill. Car park and picnic area with forest walks to Lagaville, Urie Loch, Whiting Bay and Kilmory.' There is a grassy area with picnic tables to the right of the forest track, with car parking available beside Monamore Burn.

Leave the car park and go through a **barrier gate** and cross a bridge over **Monamore Burn**. A sign on the left indicates a track for Whiting Bay and Kilmory, and this is marked as suitable for cyclists. A sign to the right indicates the 'Lagaville Walks' and the hill walk to Urie Loch. Follow the **riverside path** a short way upstream alongside Monamore Burn, then cross a **footbridge** on the right over a smaller burn. Turn left and walk upstream, passing oak, birch and other trees alongside the burn, which contrast with the clear-felled and replanted forest alongside. Climb up a few **steps** and walk alongside a wooden fence. A footbridge on the left overlooks a small waterfall in a **rocky gorge**. Don't cross the footbridge, which offers only a rapid return to the Dyemill car park.

A red arrow beside the **footbridge** points uphill for Urie Loch and care is needed in wet weather as exposed tree roots could be slippery. After passing the next **red marker** the path climbing uphill is stonier underfoot. The path pulls away from the burn on a clear-felled and replanted slope. It briefly returns to the **burn** and then enters a higher part of the forest. The path running uphill is muddy in places and is flanked with heather and later with bracken as it climbs. There is a gentler stretch, then a steeper climb. The path climbs up a **forest ride**,

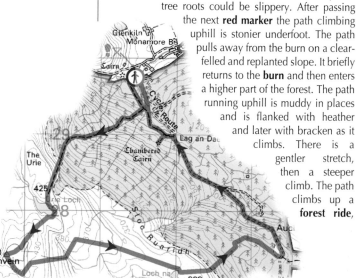

The path leading up towards Urie Lock features a good mixture of tree species

which is mostly grassy, then climbs up a steep slope of coarse grass. It cuts diagonally left across a heathery slope studded with a few boulders, running along the top edge of the forest beneath the rugged slopes of **Creag na h' Ennie**.

A final red marker post at the top corner of the forest points across a rise of squelchy moorland over 400m. The path passes a couple of boulders and then runs down to the shores of **Urie Loch**. ▶ Walk south-west from the head of Urie Loch. There is no trodden path over the heather, and the summit of **Tighvein** is not seen until at close quarters, but bears both a cairn and trig point at 458m. Views of the immediate surroundings embrace rugged, rolling moorlands. Northwards the higher mountains of the Isle of Arran are well displayed.

This is the end of the waymarked trail and anyone whose navigation is not up to scratch should consider retracing steps to the Dyemill car park. Those who can navigate confidently across bleak and **pathless moorlands** can continue and complete a rough, tough moorland and forest circuit.

A **fence** traverses the moorland slopes just south of the summit of **Tighvein**. Walk towards the fence and turn left to follow it through the heather. At a **junction** with another fence, keep left to continue. The fence leads down into a steep-sided little **valley** where a variety of flowers may be seen growing. Follow the fence up a short, steep slope onto a level moorland shoulder around 380m. Looking east-south-east across the moorland to the right, two shades of vegetation can be distinguished, separated by a **shallow ditch**. Follow this line onwards, then later continue along a rugged, heathery crest to traverse the moorland towards the lonely pool of **Loch na Leirg**.

Keep to the northern and eastern side of Loch na Leirg, then take great care to find the correct route off the moorland crest. Walk directly eastwards away from the loch to reach a rounded **moorland brow** overlooking the forested slopes falling towards Lamlash Bay and Whiting Bay. Look carefully along the edge to locate a **heathery notch**. Walk down towards the forest and pick a way through some awkward **willow scrub** on boggy ground. Look carefully for a **vague path** trodden between the trees, just to the right of a **small burn**, and continue downhill onto a clear-felled and replanted slope.

Watch carefully as the path turns left to cross a couple of **small burns** close together, where there is more awkward willow scrub, then turn right and walk slightly uphill. Take care to follow a **forest ride** straight ahead, not a broader one to the left, until another ride is reached which carries a **grassy track**. Turn right to follow this towards a large **quarry** where gravel and stone have been extracted. Keep to the right-hand side and avoid the quarry edge, then drop onto a broad and clear **forest track**. A signboard gives directions for Whiting Bay, Kilmory and Lamlash. There is a picnic table above the forest track, and a fine view of the whole of Holy Isle filling Lamlash Bay.

Turn left to follow the **forest track** downhill, then after passing a **junction** the track climbs up across a clear-felled and replanted slope. Birch trees often flank the track on the next downhill stretch. Look out for a **sign** on the left, which indicates a path leading to Meallach's Grave. The gravel path runs through trees and crosses a small **footbridge** over a little burn. It runs along a forest ride, then a **white waymark** points left uphill through the trees. A final grassy path leads to a pleasant clearing where four upright stones are located. This is **Meallach's Grave**.

Retrace steps downhill and turn left along the path at the next junction. The path reaches a small concrete **footbridge** where a small sign points the way towards the remains of **Lagaville Village**. Only a few low, mossy, tumbled walls remain, hidden deep in the forest, where the poor clachan of Lagaville was located.

LAGAVILLE

Lagaville was inhabited until the late 19th century, when the clachan was cleared. Only a few of the people were re-housed in Lamlash, while others emigrated to Canada. A monument on a green at Lamlash commemmorates the Arran Clearances. Behind the monument is a long row of terraced cottages built to accommodate people who once lived in places such as Lagaville. The Dyemill car park recalls the fact that there was once a water mill beside Monamore Burn, where cloth was finished and dyed.

Follow the path further downhill, passing a small **pond** and bench before following a burn downstream to a **footbridge**. Turn right to cross the footbridge, then turn left and follow a blue waymarked path downstream. There is a bench offering a fine view of a **waterfall** on the way downhill. At the next footbridge, do not cross, but turn right to reach a forest track. Turn left to cross a bridge over **Monamore Burn** to return to the **Dyemill** car park. Walkers without cars can easily walk along the road to reach **Lamlash**, passing the Arran Fine Foods factory at the bottom of **The Ross road**.

WALK 11
Glenashdale Falls

Distance	4.5km (2.75 miles), with an optional 1.5km (1 mile) extension.
Height gain	120m/315ft or 230m/755ft
Start/finish	Coffee Pot restaurant, Whiting Bay – grid ref. 046255
Terrain	Easy roads, forest tracks and paths, with a long flight of steep steps on the optional extension.
Refreshments	Bars, cafés and restaurants in Whiting Bay.

There is a popular, short, circular walk running round Glenashdale Falls from Whiting Bay. It can be accessed either from Ashdale Bridge, for a clockwise circuit, or from the Coffee Pot restaurant, for an anti-clockwise circuit. The latter course is chosen here, as the circuit is slightly easier in that direction. There is also an option to extend the walk towards the end by climbing a flight of steps to reach a clearing where the ancient Giant's Graves are located. As with all waterfall walks, this route lends itself to completion after a spell of heavy rain, when the falls will be at their most powerful. Walk 12 visits Glenashdale Falls on the way to a longer moorland circuit.

Start by the Coffee Pot restaurant in **Whiting Bay**, where a public footpath signpost points straight up a road indicating the way to Glenashdale Falls. The road climbs, turns right and left, climbs further uphill and passes through a **crossroads**. Another public footpath signpost offers a number of destinations, including Knockenkelly and Auchencairn. The direction for Glenashdale, however, is straight onwards. The road rises slightly, then descends to pass some **cottages** beside a burn, before climbing again. The continuation of the road is along a **clear track**.

The track passes through **gates** to reach a forest at a sign reading 'Forestry Commission Forest Walks' giving destinations including Lamlash and Kilmory. There is a **ford** to be crossed, then the forest track rises gradually. Look out for a sign on the left which reads 'Glenashdale Falls via Iron Age Fort', where a narrow path heads off downhill to the left. The path reaches a small **viewpoint** stance where there is a bench, featuring a distant view of Glenashdale Falls in a lovely mixed woodland setting.

Continue along the path, following white marker arrows, to pass the site of the **Iron Age Fort** and eventually reach the top of the **waterfalls**. There is no safe viewpoint on this side of the waterfalls, and fencing has been installed to deter visitors from getting into difficulties. Cross a **footbridge** near a picnic table and turn left to continue. A spur path off to the left, signposted as a viewpoint, leads down a flight of steps to reach the best close-up view of the **Glenashdale Falls** from a fenced stance.

GLENDASHDALE FALLS

Glenashdale was well wooded long before the Forestry Commission planted the higher slopes with conifers. The walk to Glenashdale Falls has always been a popular choice for a short, scenic stroll. The best time to view the waterfalls is of course after a spell of wet weather. A short and a long fall plunge gracefully into a deep, wooded gorge.

Admire the waterfall, then retrace steps uphill and turn left along the main path to continue. The path descends through delightfully mixed, mossy woodlands, crossing a little **footbridge**, where a slender waterfall can be seen in a rocky gorge. Cross another little **footbridge** and walk down to a **junction** of paths beside a ruined building, where there is an option to turn right and climb uphill to visit the Giants' Graves.

WALKING ON THE ISLE OF ARRAN

Optional extension

There are **337 wooden steps** climbing up the forested slope. Turn left and there is a gentler stretch, followed by another steep path to a **bench** overlooking Whiting Bay. A dark and sometimes muddy path leads into a grassy clearing where the **Giants' Graves** can be inspected.

GIANTS' GRAVES

The Giants' Graves are found in a clearing high in the forest above Whiting Bay. They are of a construction known as 'horned gallery graves'. They are believed to have been used for the burial of people of close kinship in Neolithic times, with the bodies being placed into stone chambers, which were then covered by large cairns. The 'horns' are the upright stones flanking the entrances to the graves, creating a semi-circular forecourt, which may have been a place where burial rituals were performed.

Retrace steps back down the **wooden steps** and turn right at the bottom. A clear, level path becomes a broad track, passing a couple of houses on the way out of the woods to reach the main road. Turn left along the main road, crossing **Ashdale Bridge** to return to the Coffee Pot restaurant.

WHITING BAY

Human habitation dates back thousands of years around Whiting Bay. The Giants' Graves are Neolithic and their construction suggests that there were communities in the area accustomed to working well together. At Kingscross there is a Viking burial mound. The area also has its share of stories concerning Robert the Bruce. He is said to have waited at Kingscross to see a signal lit on the Ayrshire coast, heralding his long and bitter campaign to gain the Scottish crown. Two large farmsteads called Knockenkelly and Auchencairn paid rent directly to the king for centuries. The main road around the bay dates only from 1843, and there was once a pier built out into the bay (later demolished), with tourists brought in by boats to be transferred to wagonettes. To this day the village has several hotels. A list of facilities in the village is included at the end of Walk 12.

Glenashdale Falls feature a long and a short plunge in a wooded, rocky gorge

WALK 12
Glenashdale and Loch na Leirg

Distance	10km (6 miles)
Height gain	350m/1150ft or 460m/1510ft
Start	Ashdale Bridge, Whiting Bay – grid ref. 046253
Terrain	Easy forest paths and tracks at a low level, but also an exposed pathless moorland, requiring careful navigation.

A popular short walk climbs above Whiting Bay and runs around the wooded, forested Glenashdale for a fine view of the Glenashdale Falls. This route is covered by Walk 11. Walkers can use the paths through Glenashdale to approach the bleak and empty moorlands beyond, enjoying a more ambitious walk altogether. This route involves climbing from the forest and approaching the lonely moorland pool of Loch na Leirg. Although there are trodden paths allowing walkers to reach the moors, the higher parts are quite pathless and need careful navigation, especially in mist. The descent is quite rugged at first, but becomes much easier as the route returns to Whiting Bay.

Start in **Whiting Bay**, from Ashdale Bridge at the southern end of the village. Signposts beside the bridge indicate the way along a **track** to the Giants' Graves and Glenashdale Falls. Follow the track past the last house and enter the **forest**. Another sign confirms that this is the way to the Giants' Graves and Glenashdale Falls. A little further along there is a **junction** of paths where a left turn leads to the Giants' Graves, and straight ahead leads to Glenashdale Falls. A visit to both is recommended, but you can regard the walk to the Giants' Graves as optional.

Optional extension
There are **337 wooden steps** climbing up the forested slope. Turn left and there is a gentler stretch, followed by

another steep path to a **bench** overlooking Whiting Bay.
A dark and sometimes muddy path leads into a grassy
clearing where the **Giants' Graves** can be inspected.

GIANTS' GRAVES

The Giants' Graves are found in a clearing high in the forest above Whiting
Bay. They are of a construction known as 'horned gallery graves'. They are
believed to have been used for the burial of people of close kinship in
Neolithic times, with the bodies being placed into stone chambers, which
were then covered by large cairns. The 'horns' are the upright stones flanking the entrances to the graves, creating a semi-circular forecourt, which
may have been a place where burial rituals were performed.

Retrace your steps back down the **wooden steps** and
turn left to continue further into **Glenashdale**. There is a firm
riverside path at first, then the path climbs uphill to cross a
little **footbridge** on the valley side. The path contours
through pleasantly mixed, mossy woods. Cross over another
little **footbridge**, where a slender waterfall can be seen in a
rocky gorge. A signpost points to the right, indicating a
viewpoint, down a flight of steps. This offers the best close-
up view of the **Glenashdale Falls** from a fenced stance.

GLENASHDALE FALLS

Glenashdale was well wooded long before the Forestry Commission planted
the higher slopes with conifers. The walk to Glenashdale Falls has always
been a popular choice for a short, scenic stroll. The best time to view the
waterfalls is of course after a spell of wet weather. A short and a long fall
plunge gracefully into a deep, wooded gorge.

Admire the waterfall, then retrace your steps uphill
and turn right along the main path. This crosses another
little **footbridge** and there is another fenced viewpoint
overlooking only the upper part of the waterfall. A more
substantial footbridge spans **Glenashdale Burn** above the
waterfalls and there is a picnic table beside the river.

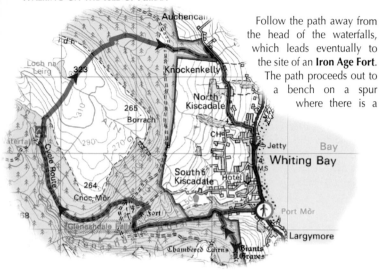

Follow the path away from the head of the waterfalls, which leads eventually to the site of an **Iron Age Fort**. The path proceeds out to a bench on a spur where there is a

viewpoint stance offering a distant view of Glenashdale Falls. Turn sharply left uphill to reach a **forest track**, then turn left again to follow it. The track bends right and climbs to a **junction**. Turn left, then right, following a cycleway marked for Kilmory. The track climbs past a few **wooden chalets**, then it roughly contours around the forested slopes of **Cnoc Mor**. Watch for a picnic table to the right of the track, where a small fenced-off waterfall can be investigated to the left, on the rushing burn of **Allt Dhepin**.

Turn right to leave the forest track and follow a **path** upstream from the waterfall. A substantial strip has been left unplanted with trees and the path has been constructed along it, roughly parallel to the **Allt Dhepin**. On reaching the edge of the forest the path expires on a rugged moorland beside the burn. Head roughly north-east from the edge of the forest, climbing up a rugged heathery slope. Look out for a **small cairn** on a heathery rise, then continue walking north-east, passing within sight of the lonely moorland pool of **Loch na Leirg**. Avoid walking too close to its outflow, where the ground is very soft and boggy.

Continue walking to reach a rounded **moorland brow** overlooking the forested slopes falling towards Lamlash Bay and Whiting Bay. Look carefully along the edge to locate a **heathery notch**. Walk down towards the forest and pick a way through some awkward **willow scrub** on boggy ground. Look carefully for a **vague path** trodden between the trees, just to the right of a **small burn**, and continue downhill onto a clear-felled and replanted slope.

Watch carefully as the path turns left to cross a couple of **small burns** close together, where there is more awkward willow scrub, then turn right and walk slightly uphill. Watch carefully to follow a forest ride straight ahead, not a broader one to the left, until another ride is reached which carries a **grassy track**. Turn right to follow this towards a large **quarry** where gravel and stone have been extracted. Keep to the right-hand side and avoid the quarry edge, then drop onto a broad and clear **forest track**. A signboard gives directions for Whiting Bay, Kilmory and Lamlash. There is a picnic table above the forest track, and a fine view of the whole of Holy Isle filling Lamlash Bay.

Loch na Leirg occupies a bleak and boggy hollow on the slopes of Tighvein

85

Walk down the **narrow forest track** signposted 'Whiting Bay via Hawthorne'. The track is mostly stony, but it can be muddy in places. It runs downhill, passing through an old **gateway** in a wall and fence. After dropping through a dark stand of mature trees the track emerges into a lighter area and finally drops down to a narrow tarmac road at **Hawthorne Farm**. Turn right to follow the road uphill and continue along a stony track. Keep to the right to pass **Knockenkelly House**, as the track descending to the left can be rather muddy. Keep straight on past **Primrose Cottage**, following the track along, then downhill, then right at a junction with another track. Houses are passed on the final run down into **Whiting Bay**. To complete the circuit, turn right along the main coastal road and walk back through the village to **Ashdale Bridge**.

WHITING BAY

Whiting Bay is a long and straggly village with two distinct halves separated by a gap. Working from north to south, features and facilities include: the Sandbraes Holiday Park, parish church, Sandbraes Park and toilets, Whiting Bay Garage, Bay Stores, Trafalgar Restaurant, Argentine Guest House, Invermay Bed and Breakfast, Burlington Hotel and restaurant, Cameronia Hotel and Chinese restaurant, Craig Ard Bed and Breakfast, Royal Arran Hotel, Whiting Bay Primary School and St. Columba's old church.

After a gap there are the following features and facilities: filling station and home improvements, Crafts of Arran, Joshua's cafe, bar and bistro, newsagent and toilets. These are followed by the Pantry restaurant, Post Office, chemist, Village Shop, village hall, putting green, Ellangowan and Mingulay Bed and Breakfasts, Corriedoon Care Home, Eden Lodge Hotel and Bar Eden, Coffee Pot restaurant, Belford Mill and the access road for View Bank House Bed and Breakfast and Whiting Bay Golf Course. At the southern end of the village is Ashdale Bridge and a caravan park.

WALK 13
Lamlash and Kingscross

Distance	14km (8.5 miles)
Height gain	270m/885ft
Start	Lamlash Parish Church – grid ref. 025309
Terrain	A rugged coastal walk, where high water should be avoided, gives way to easier paths, forest tracks and roads.
Refreshments	Bars, cafés and restaurants in Lamlash and Whiting Bay.

The sheltered waters of Lamlash Bay are well protected by the mountain-like mass of Holy Isle. Many visitors to Lamlash enjoy a stroll along the grassy green ribbon that runs around the bay between the road and shore. Some must wonder if they could walk any further, but in fact there is no coastal path to Kingscross, only a steep slope of wilderness woodland. There are, however, patches of grass and shingle beaches along the shore that may be rough underfoot; if the tide is out for the duration of the walk, there will be no problem covering the distance between Lamlash and Kingscross. Once Kingscross Point is reached, walkers can come ashore and make their way to Whiting Bay. From there it is a simple matter to climb into the forest and return to Lamlash using a broad and clear forest track.

Start at the parish church in **Lamlash** and walk south along the coastal green. When the green runs out, cross a minor road and follow a gravel path signposted for the Cordon Caravan Site. Cross a footbridge over **Benlister Burn** and note the view of Holy Isle seen across the bay from the river mouth. The path continues between masses of gorse bushes to reach another **minor road**. Turn left along the road and cross a bridge over Monamore Burn, then pass a few houses in the little settlement of **Cordon**.

At the end of the road, continue along a **track**, then veer left down a short path onto the pebbly shore of

Don't attempt this part of the walk when a high tide is expected as some parts could prove difficult to negotiate.

Lamlash Bay. Turn right to walk along the rugged shore. There is no path on the wooded slope rising inland, which is like a jungle, featuring a rich undergrowth dominated by Japanese knotweed and garlic-scented ramsons. The shore can be slippery with seaweed, but try and pick a way along **grassy patches**, though these need care too as they are pock-marked with holes. ◄

Pass a concrete **slipway** that serves a fish farm, then walk along an easier shingle beach. There are opportunities to come ashore near a couple of houses, and the rocky **Kingscross Point** is reached. Look for the remains of a Viking fort near the end of the point.

Head inland from **Kingscross Point**, rising gently through a mown, grassy area, overlooking the waters of **Whiting Bay**. Further uphill, watch for a path on the left; not the one going down towards the shore, but another one leading to a **stile** giving access to a field. Walk alongside the field and go through a **gate** into another field, then follow a path down through a wild and stony **woodland**. Another stile takes the path out of the wood, and the way ahead is flanked by masses of gorse bushes. A final stile leads down onto a **pebbly beach**.

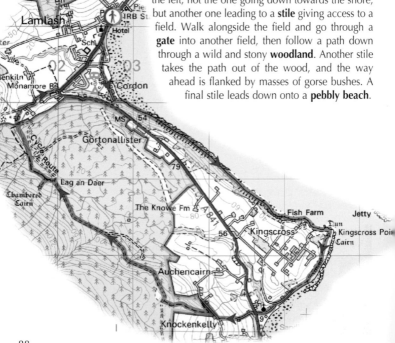

KINGSCROSS POINT

Vikings were active around the Isle of Arran from about AD800, and eventually suffered defeat at the Battle of Largs in 1263. On that occasion, the Norse fleet was moored in Lamlash Bay ahead of the battle. Arran and many other islands held by the Norse were sold to Alexander III of Scotland in 1266. The remains of a Viking fort can be studied on Kingscross Point, and Viking burial sites are known here and at nearby Lamlash.

Turn right to walk along the beach, then come ashore to follow a track and a minor road past a few houses. Eventually, the road passes the Parish Church and a sports pitch to reach the main road in the village of **Whiting Bay**. At this point there is the option of catching a bus back to Lamlash. ▶

For a list of facilities in Whiting Bay, see the end of Walk 12.

To continue the walk, cross over the main road and follow the narrow road signposted uphill as the cart track to Knockenkelly. Pass a **nursery** and walk up a wet and muddy track until a right turn can be made along a clearer track. Follow this a short way downhill, and it becomes surfaced with tarmac as it passes **Hawthorne Farm**. Turn sharp left back uphill as signposted 'Forest Path'. A clear track climbs up through the forest, crossing an open space along the way. After passing through an old **gateway** in a wall and fence, it emerges from the trees on a broad forest track near a large **quarry** where gravel and stone have been extracted. A signboard gives directions back to

The low, rocky shores of Lamlash Bay and the view north towards Goat Fell

89

Whiting Bay, as well as to Kilmory and Lamlash. There is a picnic table above the forest track, and a fine view of the whole of Holy Isle filling Lamlash Bay.

Turn right to follow the **forest track** downhill, then after passing a **junction** the track climbs up across a clear-felled and replanted slope. Birch trees often flank the track on the next downhill stretch. Look out for a **sign** on the left, which indicates a path leading to Meallach's Grave. The gravel path runs through trees and crosses a small **footbridge** over a little burn. It runs along a forest ride, then a **white waymark** points left uphill through the trees. A final grassy path leads to a pleasant clearing where four upright stones are located. This is **Meallach's Grave**.

Retrace steps downhill and turn left along the path at the next junction. The path reaches a small concrete **footbridge** where a small sign points the way towards the remains of **Lagaville Village**. Only a few low, mossy, tumbled walls remain, hidden deep in the forest, where the poor clachan of Lagaville was located.

LAGAVILLE

Lagaville was inhabited until the late 19th century, then the clachan was cleared. Only a few of the people were re-housed in Lamlash, while others emigrated to Canada. A monument on a green at Lamlash commemmorates the Arran Clearances. Behind the monument is a long row of terraced cottages built to accommodate people who once lived in places such as Lagaville.

Follow the path further downhill, passing a small **pond** and bench before following a burn downstream to a **footbridge**. Turn right to cross the footbridge, then turn left and follow a blue waymarked path downstream. There is a bench offering a fine view of a **waterfall** on the way downhill. At the next footbridge, do not cross, but turn right to reach a forest track. Turn left to cross a bridge over **Monamore Burn** to reach the **Dyemill** car park.

Continue to **The Ross road** and turn right to pass the **Dyemill Lodges** on the way to the main road and the **Arran Fine Foods** factory. Turn left along the main road, and if a bus happens to come along, then catch it to return quickly to **Lamlash**, otherwise simply walk along the road to return to the Parish Church. ▶

For a list of facilities in Lamlash, see the end of Walk 6.

WALK 14
Lagg to Kildonan Coastal Walk

Distance	8km (5 miles)
Height gain	30m/100ft
Start	Kilmory Post Office – grid ref. 956215
Finish	Kildonan Post Office – grid ref. 017213
Terrain	Rugged coastal walking with some muddy patches. Some beach walks are bouldery. The tide needs to be out at the Black Cave.
Refreshments	Lagg and Kildonan have hotels with bars and restaurants. Lagg also has a café.

The southern shores of the Isle of Arran offer a fine, rugged coastal walk with a strong feature at the Black Cave on Bennan Head. The usual approach to the Black Cave is along the coast from Kildonan, but there is another approach from Lagg. Combining these two approaches makes a good linear route and both ends of the walk have small parking spaces and linking bus services. A circular route is possible only by following the main road back from Kildonan to Lagg after completing the coastal walk, but this would be something of an anticlimax and is not particularly recommended. There is, however, a point of interest along the road where the South Bank Farm Park offers a farm trail, rare breeds and tearoom. For this walk to be completed the tide needs to be out, otherwise it is impossible to walk around Bennan Head and enter Black Cave.

WALKING ON THE ISLE OF ARRAN

Start this coastal walk at **Lagg**, beside the Kilmory Post Office, grocery and café, across the bridge from the Lagg Hotel, which was founded in 1791. A signpost points the way to Torrylin Cairn,

and a clear **gravel path** rises through a woodland and runs along the edge of a valley. Go either way at a fork in the path, as both options quickly join again. The path descends gently and swings to the left to reach a small gate. The gate gives access to **Torrylin Cairn**, the remains of which lie in a fenced enclosure.

TORRYLIN CAIRN

Much of the stonework from the 5300 year old Torrylin Cairn has been plundered as building material, leaving only a fraction of the original burial chamber and cairn behind. Note how the chamber is aligned in the direction of Ailsa Craig. The structure is characteristic of the Clyde cairns found throughout this part of Scotland. The chamber was excavated in 1900, when it was discovered that only the innermost compartment was undisturbed. The remains of six adults, a child and an infant were identified, along with a small flint tool and a fragment of a pottery bowl. The Isle of Arran had been settled for at least 2700 years by the time the Torrylin Cairn was constructed. This and similar monuments indicate the development of small, dispersed agricultural settlements with a high degree of community involvement.

Go back through the gate and continue along the path, passing a **gateway** before following a grassy track uphill towards a **farm**. The track bears left as it passes the farm, but another track on the right offers a direct line down to the beach. Turn left to walk along the beach, passing a **beach house**. The only access to a series of fields along the coast is from the beach, so there may well be **tractor tracks** along the shore. The beach becomes quite bouldery. Most of the boulders are curiously pitted and banded, and have obviously come from a couple of outcrops projecting above the sand, but there are also other large boulders that have their origins from elsewhere on the island.

A fine waterfall spills over the cliffs as the route approaches the village of Kildonan

Walk along the beach only until a **waterfall** is seen pouring through a rocky gorge. Come ashore at this point and go through a **gate** in a fence. A vague, grassy path can be followed onwards, and there are a couple more gates in fences to be passed through, and above each fence is a small waterfall. A beach of **huge, rounded boulders** is passed and the ground gets rather wet and muddy in places. Some areas have abundant growths of wild iris and mint, but later there are areas of thorny scrub too.

A prominent **igneous dyke** is passed, as well as the ruins of a drystone wall. The ground gets rougher, wetter and muddier. There are boulders poking through the ground as the path picks its way beneath a blocky cliff and a blocky, bouldery scree. There are also a couple more igneous dykes running out to sea. A **waterfall** is passed, which plunges into a small stand of trees. Immediately after fording the burn below the waterfall, a substantial upstanding outcrop is passed before the bouldery point of **Bennan Head**.

You can only head round the point safely while the tide is out, as the boulders that need to be crossed are otherwise underwater and the cliff above the waterline is sheer and hoary with lichen. Just around the corner is the **Black Cave**, which is easily entered. It has an exit at the back, but this is not recommended as an escape to the top of the cliff. The hole through which daylight enters is often damp, dripping and rather slippery.

BLACK CAVE

Before the Isle of Arran raised itself slightly from the sea after the Ice Age, as evidenced by its encircling raised beaches, the Black Cave must have been permanently full of sea water. Even now at high water the sea laps just inside the cave. A roof fall created the exit at the back of the cave, and a steep slope of bouldery debris has remained. When the sea was able to enter more of the cave in the past, this may well have been a blow-hole.

Continue walking across **large boulders**, then there is a choice of routes. Either walk carefully over the boulders uncovered by the tide, or walk at a higher level, linking bouldery and grassy areas to proceed. Neither way is particularly easier than the other, and care is needed to avoid a wrenched ankle or a fall. Some of the boulders on the shore are slippery with seaweed, while some of those above the water line are covered in a fine variety of lichens. Eventually it is better to come ashore and stay ashore.

A **path** proves to be rugged at first, but it gets better after passing a ruined **drystone wall**. The way ahead can be grassy and muddy, with more patches of wild iris, as well as rushy or brambly areas. Looking to the sea, note the large number of **igneous dykes** running across the bouldery beach. There are a couple of slender waterfalls off to the left, with a **large waterfall** seen before a gate is reached. Continue walking along the path, which gets easier and easier, passing more gates. A track is reached at the **Kildonan Stores** and post office, and again there is a waterfall just behind the buildings. You can walk through the rest of the scattered village of **Kildonan** by following the road if desired, or simply wait to catch a bus. Views to sea include the little green island of Pladda and its lighthouse, with pyramidal Ailsa Craig beyond.

KILDONAN

Kildonan derives its name from St. Donan, who arrived on the Isle of Arran with St. Columba in the 6th century. He is buried in the area and the remains of an ancient chapel are still visible. The mouldering ruins of a castle can also be inspected, though little is known of its early history. It was a property of the Stewarts, but passed to the Hamiltons in the 17th century. The present village of Kildonan is a scattered affair, and of relatively recent origin, as previously the people in the area lived in simple clachans.

Walking along the shore road reveals most of the features and facilities in the village, which from west to east include the following: Kildonan Stores and Post Office, a war memorial on an igneous dyke, car park, Breadalbane Hotel, Seal Shore Camping and Touring Site and Kildonan Hotel.

WALK 15
Kilmory Forest Circuit

Distance	16km (10 miles), with 5km (3 miles) of optional extensions.
Height gain	270m/885ft, or 580m/1900ft
Start/finish	Kilmory Post Office – grid ref. 956215
Terrain	Forest tracks and paths, mostly firm and dry, but one of the optional extensions is rough and muddy.
Refreshments	Lagg has a hotel with a bar and restaurant, as well as a café.

Much of southern Arran is under forest cover and the walking tends to be rather similar in many places. However, there is an interesting forested circuit north of the village of Kilmory, where farm tracks link with a series of forest tracks. There are also options to make diversions to look for an ancient stone circle and a burial cairn hidden deep in the forest. The walk can be conveniently started from the main road at Kilmory, near the Torrylin Creamery, but it is perhaps better to start from Lagg, which offers food and drink and gives walkers the option of including the Torrylin Cairn in addition to the forest walk. The circuit described is essentially low level, firm and dry, but one optional extension can be rough and muddy, especially in wet weather.

Start at **Lagg**, where the Lagg Hotel, founded in 1791, stands on one side of a bridge, while the post office, grocery and café stand on the other side. Follow the road winding uphill from the post office, passing the **Kilmory Public Hall**, toilets and Kilmory Primary School. Look out for the Island Porcelain building on the left, then later turn left where a narrow road is signposted for the Kilmory Workshop and parish church. The road runs along and downhill to reach **Kilmory parish church**.

A track is signposted for the Kilmory Workshop just below the church. The track runs downhill a short way and crosses a bridge over **Kilmory Water**, then climbs uphill, partly surfaced in concrete and flanked by hedges as it passes a series of fields. The Kilmory Workshop is at the top of the track at **Cloined**, where

woodwork and pottery crafts may be inspected. Cars using the rough track to visit the workshop have a small parking space alongside.

The track proceeds beyond **Cloined** and the Kilmory Workshop, descending gently and still flanked by hedges, but it is now grassy for the most part. The track reaches a forest that is mostly clear-felled and replanted, then rises to a gravel **turning space** where a clear, firm **forest track** continues straight ahead. The track passes the isolated farmstead of **Achaleffen**, which is no more than a house, outbuildings, small field and a little waterwheel. Walk straight past Achaleffen and keep following the forest track.

Optional extension

A forest track on the left is signposted for the **Achaleffen Standing Stones**. A short detour to visit the stones simply involves following the track uphill. Four blocky stones stand in a little clearing to the left. Although signposted, they are not apparent until close at hand.

Anyone not making the detour can continue straight along the lower forest track. Walk along the lower track and cross a burn called the **Allt an t-Sluice**. Avoid another track on the right and continue walking to reach a **junction**. A sign points left along a track, indicating a cross-island cycleway to Whiting Bay and Lamlash. Another sign points to the right indicating the way to Kilmory.

Optional extension

Turn left up the track as signposted for Càrn Bàn and Whiting Bay. Further up the track, turn left again as signposted for Càrn Bàn, and follow the track until a **turning space** is reached. At this point, follow a **path** gently downhill across a rugged, clear-felled slope. The path later rises gently from a waymark post and eventually reaches **Càrn Bàn** via a grassy path that can be wet and muddy in places. A sign offers a few details about the site, which is revealed as a bouldery burial mound whose upright entrance stones have been toppled. Retrace steps afterwards back to the lower **track junction**.

From the lower **track junction**, follow the track as signposted for Kilmory, leaving the forest and passing heathery ground around the isolated farmstead of **Achareoch**. The track keeps left to avoid the farm then drops down to cross a **burn**. It then runs uphill and later runs gradually downhill in a largely clear-felled area of

CÀRN BÀN

Hidden in a forest clearing, reached only by following a forest ride, this bouldery Neolithic chambered tomb was used for communal burial about 5300 years ago. A Mesolithic hunting camp has also been discovered nearby, taking signs of human activity on the Isle of Arran back 8000 years. The main burial chamber was excavated in 1902 and discovered to be divided into four compartments. Small fragments of bone and two stone tools were retrieved. A possible second burial chamber at the lower end of the cairn has not been excavated. The existence of a burial cairn of these proportions, and their obvious frequent use indicates that the inhabitants of Arran at the time were living in fairly well-structured communities with a great sense of purpose.

forest. The track later has forest to the right and **heather moorland** to the left. Looking back later, a Forestry Commission sign gives destinations all the way back to Whiting Bay and Lamlash. After a fairly level run the track drops downhill and is flanked by gorse bushes.

Turn right along a **farm track**, which is firm and dry for only a short distance. Its continuation, straight onwards and downhill is wet and muddy; a sort of trough between hedges. There is another firm and dry track passing **Kilmory Farm House**, and when this suddenly turns to the left a rougher track continues straight on. The rougher track runs down to a minor road beside **Kilmory parish church**, and the minor road leads back to the main road. A short detour left along the main road leads to the **Torrylin Creamery**.

TORRYLIN CREAMERY

The Torrylin Creamery, or Arran Creamery, stands beside the main road in Kilmory and is open to visitors. Around 10 dairy farms supply milk to the creamery, where traditional Arran Dunlop cheeses are made by hand. The process can be observed from a viewing gallery, and products can be bought at the adjoining cheese shop. When the creamery opened in 1947 the entire Royal Family paid a visit.

The Lagg Hotel, which dates from 1791, offers food, drink and accommodation

Turn right along the main road to return directly to **Lagg**. Alternatively, turn right and almost immediately left to follow a **farm track** towards the sea. Keep right at a junction to follow the track in front of a farm overlooking the sea. Continue along the **grassy track**, which runs down through a **gateway** before climbing slightly. There is a small gate on the right at the **Torrylin Cairn**. Inspect the burial cairn (see Walk 14 for details) then continue along the path as it contours round above a **wooded valley**. There is a slight ascent on this clear path, then at a fork you can go either way, as the paths join again later. A final descent leads to the post office and café at **Lagg**. The Lagg Hotel is just along the main road, across a bridge.

WALK 16
Sliddery and Cnocan Donn

Distance	13km (8 miles)
Height gain	330m/1080ft
Start/finish	Sliddery – grid ref. 931229
Terrain	Roads, tracks, a rugged moorland walk and a bouldery coastal walk with some good paths.
Refreshments	None closer than Blackwaterfoot or Lagg.

Cnocan Donn is a hill between Sliddery and Blackwaterfoot, which is half rugged moorland and half forest. It provides exceptional views in fine weather for such a lowly height. Walkers who cross the hill can descend to Kilpatrick, then either catch a bus or pick a way back around Brown Head to return to Sliddery. The return route uses a patchy, rugged coastal path. There are features of interest at either end, such as the Preaching Cave near Kilpatrick and Torr A' Chaisteal Dun at Corriecravie. There are no real facilities along the road apart from a couple of bed and breakfast establishments and regular bus services.

Sliddery is a little village on a bend in the main coastal road between Blackwaterfoot and Kilmory. There is something of a crossroads on the bend, with a track running downhill and a **minor road** running uphill opposite a small red postbox. Follow the minor road uphill, passing a handful of houses and farms. The road rises, falls and rises gently again to a **cattle grid**. Turn left to follow the road to a **farmyard**, then turn right along a clear track running towards another farm called **Corriecravie Moor**. Walk only as far as a rise on the track, where there is a **gate** on the left. This gives access to a rugged moorland walk alongside **Kilpatrick Forest**.

Walk uphill alongside the **forest fence**, or some distance away from it, to make use of a series of vague paths. There is tussocky grass, a little bog, an abundance of heather and bracken on the slope, as well as a scattering of boulders. A short detour away from the forest fence can include the undistinguished top of **Cnoc Reamhar** at 225m. Walk back to the forest fence to go through a **gate** in an electric fence, then follow the forest fence across a squelchy gap and over a heathery rise. There is another descent to another rather wet gap, where four fences join in a swamp. Straight ahead rise the heathery slopes of **Cnocan Donn**, crowned by a trig point at 219m. From this lowly eminence, there is actually an extensive view. The highest peaks of northern Arran stretch from the Pirnmill Hills to those around Glen Rosa, crowned by Goat Fell. The lower hills and moorlands of southern Arran stretch from Ard Bheinn to Tighvein. Ailsa Craig and the coast of Ayr and Galloway can be seen, along with Antrim, Kintyre and Jura.

Head back towards the **forest fence** and continue walking downhill. There is an easy, bulldozed strip beside the forest fence, leading down to a **gateway** on the main coastal road. Turn right along the road as if walking to Blackwaterfoot.

The road bends suddenly to the right and drops down to **Kilpatrick**. Just opposite a small car park, turn left through a **gate** to follow a track down to the shore. Turn left again to walk along a **grassy strip** beside a bouldery beach at the foot of a low cliff line. There are a couple of caves in the low cliff line, including the **Preaching Cave**.

Good grazing for livestock is available in the gentle pastures around Kilpatrick

PREACHING CAVE

The Preaching Cave is a fairly spacious, smoke-blackened cave cut into the low cliff-line below Kilpatrick. It is said to have been used for church services and there are also stories of it being used as a schoolroom at a time when the area was very poor.

There is a good grassy **path** to follow for a while, but it gets more and more overgrown later with grass, heather, bracken, brambles and even honeysuckle and clumps of thrift. Transfer to the **bouldery beach** to continue, taking care while hopping from boulder to

103

A rugged walk along a raised beach leads from Kilpatrick back towards Sliddery

boulder. Looking uphill and along the cliff, little can be seen of the road, though it is very close and traffic may be heard. Looking ahead, only one corner of the road can be seen, while down on the shore around that point the walking becomes easier again. Watch for the **yellow paint** marks that reveal a short-cut up to the road, if one is needed.

It is possible to walk along a narrow, **grassy path** again, although it can feel cobbly underfoot in places, as the raised beach isn't far beneath the grass. There is a view of Ailsa Craig ahead, while out to sea seals may be hauled out basking on large boulders. Some wet and muddy parts of the path are flanked by wild iris. Drift inland from the shore along a broader, **cobbly path**, but not the tractor track, along the foot of a slope of bracken overlooked by a **white house**. When this path reaches a **gate** into a field, detour to the right around the corner of a fence to continue. The path runs out beside a large **reedbed** followed by a grassy area studded with boulders. Cross the tangled end of a fence on the beach, then walk past more reeds, before turning left through a **gate**.

A line of wild iris in a field marks the course of a small **burn**, which is followed upstream. Rising ahead is the prominent knoll of **Torr A' Chaisteal**, which has a grassy track slicing across its face. Follow the track uphill to have a look at an information board explaining about this ancient dun.

TORR A' CHAISTEAL DUN

The natural grassy knoll at Torr A' Chaisteal bears the remains of a thick-walled dun which was built around 1800 years ago. The 'dun' was a defended farmstead, situated next to an area of good agricultural land, yet close to the resources offered by the sea. The interior was partially excavated in the 19th century, producing human bones, a stone quern, pieces of haematite iron ore and midden material.

The grassy track becomes vague later, but it climbs along the edge of fields overlooking a **valley** full of hawthorns and other trees. When a cottage is reached at **Corriecravie**, cross over a stile to reach the main road. Turn right to follow the road over a rise, then descend to finish back in **Sliddery**. Bear in mind that buses can be caught at Corriecravie or Sliddery.

WALK 17
Tighvein and Glenscorrodale

Distance	13km (8 miles)
Height gain	480m/1575ft
Start/finish	Glenscorrodale – grid ref. 963279
Terrain	Mostly rugged, pathless, heather moorlands and bog, with a potentially awkward river crossing.
Refreshments	None closer than Lamlash and Lagg.

To many walkers, Tighvein seems unapproachable. Maps suggest that it is flanked on all sides by pathless, featureless moorlands, and this is at least partly true. It also appears, from a study of the map, to be almost surrounded by forestry plantations, yet it is still possible to side-step them and enjoy the best of the wild moorlands. While paths may be few, the summit can be approached from any direction simply by climbing uphill until there is nothing left to climb. Leaving the summit on this walk can be simplified by following the remains of a prominent fence across the moors. There is a ford along this route and this may be difficult to cross during wet weather. The whole circuit is based around the remote Buddhist retreat centre at Glenscorrodale. The only public transport through the glen is a Post Bus service. Judicious use of it could save walking 5km (3 miles) along the road through the glen.

The Buddhist retreat centre at **Glenscorrodale** is nominally the starting point, though parking is quite limited nearby. Follow **The Ross road** towards the forested head of the glen, passing occasional small parking spaces and **picnic tables** as the road twists and turns as it climbs. A **derelict building** will be noticed off to the right. There is a **cattle grid** at the top of The Ross road, at 285m, but don't cross it. Leave the road a little earlier by cutting sharply down to the right. There is a narrow, boggy **path** leading into the forest, obviously used by quad bikes. Walk straight over a broad **forest ride**, then head straight uphill along another ride. Turn right along one more forest ride, still following the quad bike track. The wheel marks reveal an exit to the left, passing between the trees to emerge onto a heathery slope. Walk steeply uphill following the vague track on the rugged slopes of **Gar Bheinn**, until the trail expires. The gradient eases, but the moorland remains rugged and pathless towards the broad rise of **Cnoc Dubh** and onwards to Tighvein. The heather cover is broken only by a few grassy areas, with even fewer small boulders poking through, and many channels of squelchy sphagnum moss. Side-step the channels where possible, but keep the ultimate objective of Tighvein in line.

The summit of **Tighvein** has two distinct tops; one with a trig point at 458m and the other with a cairn. Views take in the immediate bleak moorland surroundings and extend to embrace the mountainous northern half of the Isle of Arran. Just beyond the summit is the line of a **ruined fence**, featuring decaying posts and straggly, broken wires. Walk towards the fence and turn right. The **fenceposts** form a continuous line leading westwards across the moorland and are a great help with navigation away from Tighvein in poor visibility.

A **narrow ditch** accompanies the fence as it runs down a rugged moorland slope. Beware of any bits of wire that might be tangled in the grass and heather. A **burn** has to be crossed in a little valley, then the line of the fence runs along the edge of a **forest** for part of the next ascent. There is a stretch of minor ups and downs across the rugged moorland slopes of **Cnoc Lean na Meine**, before a more continuous descent commences. A junction is reached with another well-maintained fence and it is necessary to pass through a **gateway** at that point. Continue following the fence straight downhill, running alongside another stand of **forest**. A point is eventually reached where the fence turns left and is followed no further.

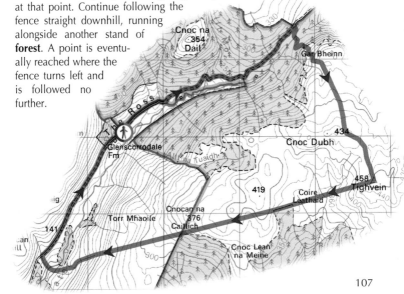

107

The broad moorland slopes surrounding Tighvein as seen across Glenscorrodale

Leave the course of the fence at the **corner**, navigating straight onwards across a rugged, pathless moorland slope. There may be a few sheep paths that can be linked to provide a good footing across the heather, but these are not continuous and may ultimately lead off-course. The aim is to chart a course towards the ruined clachan of Gargadale, leaving the gently sloping moorland slopes and dropping a little more steeply to get there.

The heather gives way to more grassy slopes as a **shallow valley** full of tree scrub is entered. There is a landmark across the valley in the shape of a rectangular stone-walled **sheepfold**, while further down the valley, across a small burn, the ruined houses and walls of **Gargadale** eventually become visible, and may be explored.

GARGADALE

Gargadale's gaunt ruins are all that survive of a small clachan tucked away in a fold in the hillside. There is rather more shape and form to these ruins than there is to many other deserted villages around the Isle of Arran, as more stone seems to have been used in its construction, rather than 'blacksod' constructions of peat. Unfortunately, unlike some of the other settlements, little is known about the fate of the tenants who were cleared from the land, although it has been suggested that they may have gone to Canada and settled at Cahleur Bay near Prince Edward Island.

Continue downhill and the remains of an old track fording **Sliddery Water** can be distinguished on either side of the river. Wet feet are to be expected at this point, while in wet weather a crossing may not actually be possible. Ford the river and climb uphill to join **The Ross road**. (If the river cannot be forded safely, then continue downstream to reach a road bridge at the next farm. Wise walkers would do well to check the flow of water in the river before starting this walk.) Turn right to follow The Ross road. The isolated Buddhist retreat centre at **Glenscorrodale** is the only building along the road, so when it is seen ahead, the end of the walk is in sight.

GLENSCORRODALE

Formerly Glenscorrodale was a remote 'steading' or small farm, with a few outbuildings. It was once the home of Scotland's First Minister, Jack McConnell. The Buddhist community of Holy Isle acquired the site and demolished the old farmhouse. New buildings were erected, while the old outbuildings were refurbished. The site has been renamed as Samye Dechen Shing, or 'valley of the pervading bliss', and operates as a retreat centre, complementing the retreat centre in the old lighthouse keeper's cottages on Holy Isle. Thousands of trees have been planted in what was formerly a rather bare, sheep-grazed part of the glen.

WALK 18
The Ross and Cnoc a' Chapuill

Distance	16km (10 miles)
Height gain	400m/1310ft
Start	Glenscorrodale – grid ref. 963279
Terrain	Roads and a vague track, but also extensive and pathless rugged moorlands.
Refreshments	None closer than Lamlash and Lagg.

The Ross road threads through Glenscorrodale, and the only public transport is a Post Bus service. Most of the upper parts of the dale have been forested, but plenty of land remains open, both along the length of the dale and on the higher moors. This walk takes a look at the extensive unforested moorlands to the north of Glenscorrodale, crossing the broad and pathless slopes of Cnoc a' Chapuill. The road is used at the beginning and end through Glenscorrodale, and the Post Bus could be used to omit a good 5km (3 miles). An old track is used to access the higher moorlands, and a couple of fences later form useful guides, but the highest parts of the route are really only for competent navigators, especially in misty weather.

nally the starting point, though parking is quite limited nearby. You could park anywhere along **The Ross road** between its highest point and the farm of Glenree, or use the Post Bus and start walking anywhere along the road. Walk away from Glenscorrodale by following the road down through the glen. The road is unfenced and traverses some rugged slopes overlooking **Sliddery Water**. Later, fences are noticed off to the right on the slopes of **Burican Hill**, enclosing three large fields.

When the access track to the farm of **Glenree** is reached beside a stand of trees on the right, turn sharply right through a gate to follow a **grassy track**. The track passes through the three large fields, but the way ahead is sometimes vague. Look ahead to spot **three gates**, all slightly off to the left, and a fine track becomes apparent which crosses a burn flowing into the **Allt Burican** near some trees. While the course of the track is very clear at this point, its continuation still needs care. Follow the track uphill and it bends to the left, becoming no more than a vague groove running through grass, heather and bracken. It swings to the right and proceeds roughly northwards across the broad slopes of **Boguille**.

The track rises very gently across the moorland slope and cuts a fairly clear line across the slope at times. Quad bikes have been ridden alongside and a few walkers have trodden a narrow path. Only one small **burn** of any

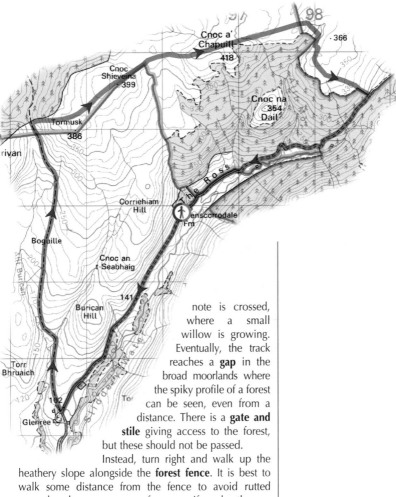

note is crossed, where a small willow is growing. Eventually, the track reaches a **gap** in the broad moorlands where the spiky profile of a forest can be seen, even from a distance. There is a **gate and stile** giving access to the forest, but these should not be passed.

Instead, turn right and walk up the heathery slope alongside the **forest fence**. It is best to walk some distance from the fence to avoid rutted ground and cross an area of more uniform heather on **Tormusk**. Drift further and further away from the fence to gain height, crossing more hummocky and awkward ground on **Cnoc Shieveina**. There are channels of squelchy sphagnum moss to be crossed, and no trodden

A lonely moorland pool on Cnoc a' Chapuill and a distant glimpse of Goat Fell

paths anywhere. Look out for a **small cairn** at 399m overlooking a broad moorland gap. Descend to cross the **gap**, which proves to be quite richly vegetated. A **fence** also needs to be crossed, then any route can be chosen up the broad, heathery slopes beyond.

Clear weather is a distinct advantage on this broad, pathless moorland. There is nothing to mark the 419m summit of **Cnoc a' Chapuill** and the moorland slopes spread in all directions. There are distant views of the jagged peaks of northern Arran, while closer to hand across Glenscorrodale is Tighvein and more extensive moorlands. Head roughly east-north-east along the hummocky **moorland crest**, keeping well above the forested slopes of Glenscorrodale. When a **fence** is reached, cross it and turn right to follow it.

The fence runs alongside a **forest** for a short while, then it turns right and zigzags on the moorland slope. There is a climb onto a moorland hump, then a swing to the left before a descent, which runs alongside another part of the forest. The fence runs straight down to the top of **The Ross road**. Keep left of the fence for a while before joining the road, then turn right to follow the road across a **cattle grid**. The rest of the route is simply a matter of following the road back down to Glenscorrodale. The road runs through forest most of the way, but there are views along the length of the glen, as well as a handful of picnic tables. Just after a **derelict building** is noticed on the left, the road twists and turns downhill. A more level stretch of road returns to the remote Buddhist retreat centre at **Glenscorrodale**, and the end is in sight from the time you see the buildings.

GLENSCORRODALE

It is said that a giant called Scorrie lived in the glen, hence the name of Glenscorrodale. The only road is The Ross road, which was constructed in 1821. Its construction involved local tenants either giving six days of labour towards the project, or making a payment towards the work. Afterwards, tenants were obliged to give three days of labour towards its maintenance, or towards the later building of bridges.

WALK 19
Shiskine and Clauchan Glen

Distance	11km (6.5 miles)
Height gain	350m/1150ft
Start/finish	Shiskine – grid ref. 913299
Terrain	Mostly good tracks and paths through farmland and forest, but also some rugged moorland walking.
Refreshments	None closer than Blackwaterfoot or the Old Mill Coffee House at the Balmichael Visitor Centre.

A varied circular walk is available from the village of Shiskine, which includes a number of fairly clear paths and tracks. The route runs up through Clauchan Glen, climbs through forest, then takes in some fine heather moorlands and a scenic loch, before descending through forest and running down through farmland. The walk starts and finishes on The String road, which was surveyed and designed by Thomas Telford, linking Blackwaterfoot and Brodick. A little accommodation and a campsite is available at Shiskine, along with regular bus services, but if any other facilities are needed it is necessary to travel to nearby Blackwaterfoot or over to Brodick.

Leave the village of **Shiskine** by walking along **The String road** in the direction of Brodick. The road crosses a **bridge** outside the village, then passes the **Bridgend campsite** at the foot of Clauchan Glen. Turn right up a narrow tarmac road beside the campsite. The road features a line of leaning beech trees to the left and a **burial ground** to the right. The tarmac ends at a small parking space beside the burial ground and a gravel track runs uphill between fields and a forest, passing a covered reservoir, to reach a little cottage called **Sron na Carraige**.

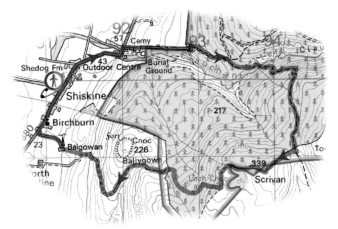

Pass a **barrier gate** and follow the track into a clear-felled and replanted forest. The track bends as it climbs, then after a straight stretch, look out for a **narrow track** heading off to the right. The track drops down to a bouldery ford over the Clauchan Water in **Clauchan Glen**. A grassy track zigzags up from the ford, with heathery banks alongside, and occasional peeps through the trees into the glen. There is a broad slope of heather at a higher level, where a **marker post** for Glenree stands on a bend. There is a muddy stretch, then the track crosses a small **burn**. There is a slight descent before a gentle ascent to a **gate and stile** at the edge of the forest.

Do not cross the stile, but turn right to walk between the forest and a fence. A track made by quad bikes climbs uphill on the slopes of **Scrivan**. Anyone crossing the fence and climbing to the 341m summit can enjoy views stretching beyond Ard Bheinn, taking in some of the larger hills to the north. The forest fence turns right where there is a large area of squelchy sphagnum moss, then leads down towards **Loch Cnoc an Loch**, which features two little islands. Turn left to walk between the shore of the loch and the edge of the forest, following the wheel marks left by quad bikes on the rugged moorland. These marks may prove difficult to spot, but watch carefully to

The Pirnmill Hills are in view during the descent to Ballygown and Shiskine

find where they continue down from the moorland into a **forest ride**.

Follow the track down along the **forest ride**, then turn left to contour across the forested slope. A right turn leads down along another **heathery ride**, with another slight right turn taking the track down alongside a little **burn**. There is a **gate** in the forest fence, from where the track proceeds more clearly through a small valley between **Cnoc Ballygown**, crowned with the remains of a hill fort, and Beinn Tarsuinn.

Follow the track through the valley, and cross the little **burn** a couple of times. Heather and bracken give way to more grassy ground when the track passes through a **gate**. Follow a fence onwards to reach another **gate**, where the track swings sharply right. As the track cuts down across the slope, it is often flanked by dense gorse bushes, and views extend across Blackwaterfoot and Machrie to the higher hills. Go through another **gate** beside a line of beech trees and turn left. The track bends right and left on the way down to the farm of **Ballygown**, passing through two more gates to reach the farmyard.

Follow the farm access track off to the right to descend to the road. Turn right along the road to walk back through the village of Shiskine. Pass the **parish church** (or 'red kirk'), which is resplendently red among the green fields, and Shiskine Primary School. There are a number of houses straggling along the road through **Shiskine**, and a single bed and breakfast at Croftlea.

SHISKINE

The name Shiskine refers to marshy ground, yet there is an expanse of good farmland in the area. There is a story relating that St. Molaise brought Christianity to Shiskine and that his remains were interred in Clauchan Glen. There is also a tradition that a pilgrimage path ran from Shiskine, up through Clauchan Glen, over to Lamlash and so by ferry to Holy Isle. Up until the 1930s Shiskine was a very industrious village, with a number of shops and businesses, but now it is a quiet place with only one bed and breakfast, a nearby campsite and a handful of self-catering properties. There are regular coast-to-coast bus services through the village.

WALK 20
Ballymichael and Ard Bheinn

Distance	13km (8 miles)
Height gain	600m/1970ft
Start/finish	Balmichael Visitor Centre – grid ref. 925315
Terrain	A forest track and path at the start, otherwise rugged, pathless moorland needing careful navigation in mist. The route ends on a road.
Refreshments	Old Mill Coffee House at the Balmichael Visitor Centre.

Beinn Bhreac and Ard Bheinn are rough and pathless hills rising east of The String road at Ballymichael. Access is most easily gained via the forest track in Clauchan Glen, but after that the walking is rough and tough. There are few trodden paths, no easy ways to cross over the two summits, and in misty weather accurate navigation is essential. In order to make a complete circular walk, a stretch of The String road, surveyed and designed by Thomas Telford, is followed through Ballymichael. There is also the chance to include a tour of the Balmichael Visitor Centre at the start or finish of the walk.

There is hardly any room to park beside the road around **Ballymichael**. The car park at the Balmichael Visitor Centre is for patrons only, but permission could be sought there. Anyone arriving by bus will of course have no parking problems. Follow the road away from the **Balmichael Visitor Centre** as if heading for the nearby village of Shiskine. Turn left up a narrow tarmac road at the **Bridgend Campsite** at the foot of Clauchan Glen. This road features a line of leaning beech trees to the left and a **burial ground** to the right. The tarmac ends at a small parking space beside the burial ground and a gravel track runs uphill between fields and a forest, passing a covered reservoir, to reach a little cottage called **Sron na Carraige**.

Pass a **barrier gate** and follow the track into a clear-felled and replanted forest. The track bends as it climbs. After a straight stretch, a narrow track heads off to the right, but keep to the **main track** as it climbs a little further uphill. When there is a sharp bend to the left, turn right instead, following an older, **grassy track** as it winds uphill past a **small quarry**. The old track cuts out a loop of the main track, which is rejoined at a higher level. Turn right to continue ascending gently, reaching the top of the track beside another small quarry.

The track begins to descend gently towards **Clauchan Water** in Clauchan Glen. Don't go all the way down to the river, as the vegetation cover is too dense and awkward. Look instead for a **gravel ramp** rising to

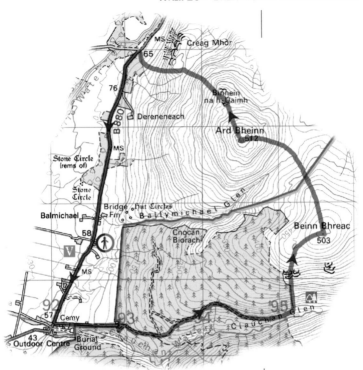

the left, giving
access to a rugged **forest ride**. Forge a way along the ride
to reach the edge of the forest, then turn left to walk
uphill alongside the remains of the **forest fence**. The
vegetation cover on the lower slopes of Beinn Bhreac is
remarkably varied, comprising bracken, grass, heather
and a host of flowering plants. This makes the ascent
interesting, but also rather difficult, and it is best to walk
some distance from the line of the forest fence.

When a **corner** of the forest fence is reached, bear
slightly to the right and climb straight up the open slope.
There is tough heather cover, broken by a few areas of
boulders. At a higher level the gradient eases and there
is mixed grass and heather cover. Go through a **small**

119

Views northwards stretch from Ard Bheinn and the Pirnmill Hills to Beinn Nuis, Glen Rosa and Goat Fell. In a southerly arc, look out for Holy Isle, Tighvein, Ailsa Craig, Antrim and Kintyre, with Jura beyond.

gate in a fence and walk along a broad shoulder where there is a **pool**, then make the final ascent to the broad summit of **Beinn Bhreac**. There is a stony cairn at 503m situated amid low heathery peat hags. ◀

Descend roughly northwards from the broad moorland summit of **Beinn Bhreac**, down a gentle slope of heather, grass and low peat hags. The ground becomes steeper and it is best to drift to the left towards a broad gap. A few boulders and rock outcrops are passed then the **broad gap**, around 370m, proves to be squelchy with sphagnum moss. Once across the gap, begin climbing fairly steeply, and it is best to drift a little more to the left. The ground becomes predominantly heathery and there are some boulders and rocky outcrops to pass. The summit of **Ard Bheinn** bears a trig point at 512m inside a circular stone shelter. There is also a cairn nearby.

Descend roughly northwards from the top of **Ard Bheinn**, then make a slight drift to the left. The aim is to pick up and follow a broad, hummocky ridge, which ends in a dome bearing a cairn. This is **Binnein**

The steep and rugged slopes of Ard Bheinn as seen from The String road

na h-Uaimh and the underlying rock is a bouldery conglomerate. Head west, then quickly swing north-west to start the descent, looking carefully down the slope to avoid steep ground or rocky outcrops. It is possible to pick a way down steep heathery ground, drifting to the right to enter a little valley behind the hump of **Creag Mhor**. The upper floor of the valley is a bit wet and bears bog myrtle.

The final part of the descent is quite short, but it is very tough underfoot and needs special care. Stay on the northern side of the **Allt nan Dris**, away from both the Derneneach Stone Quarry and the forest which can be seen below. Heather gives way to areas of bracken and boulders, which needs to be taken slowly and carefully. At a lower level, there is an ankle-wrenching slope of tussocky grass and more bracken. Aim to reach The String road to the right of the **forest**. There is a fence to cross near a road junction, where there is also a fine red sandstone **pillar box**.

Turn left along **The String road** and walk between the forest and a series of fields. Pass the access roads for the Derneneach Stone Quarry and **Derneneach Farm**. The road is then flanked on both sides by fields. After passing **Bridge Farm**, which is to the left of the road, the **Balmichael Visitor Centre** is off to the right of the road.

BALMICHAEL VISITOR CENTRE

Based on a former farm complex, the Balmichael Visitor Centre includes a number of attractions around a fine courtyard. The Old Mill Coffee House serves snacks and refreshments. There are craft shops, an antique shop and toilets. For children, there is a playground and a quad biking circuit. Quad biking tours over nearby hills, including Beinn Bhreac and Ard Beinn, are offered to adults and accompanied older children. Helicopter tours around the Isle of Arran are also available from Arran Heli-Tours. You can choose one of their standard short flights, a complete circuit around the island, or negotiate and plan a special exploratory flight anywhere. For details of flights ☎ 01770 860526 or 860326.

WALK 21
The String and Beinn Bhreac

Distance	12km (7.5 miles)
Height gain	600m/2165ft
Start/finish	Glenloig, The String road – grid ref. 946351
Terrain	A forest path and rugged, pathless moorlands needing careful navigation in mist.
Refreshments	None closer than the Old Mill Coffee House at the Balmichael Visitor Centre.

There are wild, empty moorlands and hills to the south of The String road. Farmland and forestry makes access difficult in places, but this particular walk uses a rugged forest path through Glen Craigag. Practically the whole walk is over rough, tough, pathless hill and moorland slopes, with the circuit finishing with a road walk at the end. Parking is very limited beside The String road, but there are regular bus services between Brodick and Blackwaterfoot. The route takes in three summits – A' Chruach, Beinn Bhreac and Ard Bheinn – which are all arranged in a circuit around Glen Craigag.

Parking on The String road is quite limited, but there is a small car park opposite the former farmstead of **Glenloig**, which is the last habitation seen when travelling up The String road towards Brodick, or the first seen on the way down from the highest part of the road. A Forestry Commission sign reads 'Glenloig', and although there is a path heading into the glen from the car park, it goes nowhere and should not be used. Walk to a nearby **gateway** to find another path heading into the glen.

The whole of the eastern side of **Glen Craigag** has been forested, but there is a single **ride** through it that has been left unplanted. While this ride bears a vague, trodden **path**, it is also covered in bracken, tussocky grass

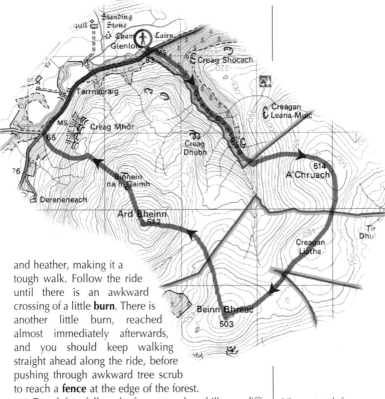

and heather, making it a tough walk. Follow the ride until there is an awkward crossing of a little **burn**. There is another little burn, reached almost immediately afterwards, and you should keep walking straight ahead along the ride, before pushing through awkward tree scrub to reach a **fence** at the edge of the forest.

Turn left to follow the fence steeply uphill on a difficult slope of **deep heather**. Cross the fence at some convenient point, then head roughly eastwards across the rugged, pathless moorlands. The gradient eases as height is gained, and the heather is less of a drag on the feet. Aim for the summit of **A' Chruach**; a broad grass and heather rise bearing a **small cairn** at 515m. ▶

Head due southwards in the direction of Ailsa Craig along the broad **moorland crest**. There is a trace of a path, but not much, and not enough to follow confidently in mist. After crossing the next broad **moorland gap**, drift to the right to cross the broad, bleak moorland summit of

Views stretch from the high peaks of northern Arran to the extensive moorlands of southern Arran, taking in the Ayr and Galloway coasts, Antrim and Kintyre. Islands in view include Cumbrae, Holy Isle, Ailsa Craig and Jura.

The mountains of northern Arran seen between A' Chruach and Beinn Bhreac

Creagan Liatha at 490m, where there are plenty of peat hags. The next gap on the moorland crest is very broad and gentle, but it is also abundantly boggy and covered in grass, sphagnum moss and peat hags. It is best avoided altogether by keeping to the northern slope of the moors, overlooking **Glen Craigag**. After passing somewhat below the gap, a firmer ascent can be made on the slopes of **Beinn Bhreac**. There is a stony cairn on top at 503m situated amid low heathery peat hags.

Descend roughly northwards from the broad moorland summit of Beinn Bhreac, down a gentle slope of heather, grass and low peat hags. The ground becomes steeper and it is best to drift to the left towards a broad gap. A few boulders and rock outcrops are passed then the **broad gap**, around 370m, proves to be squelchy with sphagnum moss. Once across the gap, begin climbing fairly steeply, and it is best to drift a little more to the left. The ground becomes predominantly heathery and there are some boulders and rocky outcrops to pass. The summit of **Ard Bheinn** bears a trig point at 514m inside a circular stone shelter. There is also a cairn nearby.

Descend roughly northwards from the top of **Ard Bheinn**, then make a slight drift to the left. The aim is to pick up and follow a broad, hummocky ridge, which ends in a dome bearing a cairn. This is **Binnein na h-Uaimh** and the underlying rock is a bouldery conglomerate. Head west, then quickly swing north-west to start the descent, looking carefully down the slope to avoid steep ground or rocky outcrops. It is possible to pick a way down steep heathery ground, drifting to the right to enter a little valley behind the hump of **Creag Mhor**. The upper floor of the valley is a bit wet and bears bog myrtle.

The final part of the descent is quite short, but it is very tough underfoot and needs special care. Stay on the northern side of the **Allt nan Dris**, away from both the Derneneach Stone Quarry and the forest which can be seen below. Heather gives way to areas of bracken and boulders, which needs to be taken slowly and carefully. At a lower level, there is an ankle-wrenching slope of tussocky grass and more bracken. Aim to reach The String road to the right of the **forest**. There is a fence to cross near a road junction, where there is also a fine red sandstone **pillar box**.

Turn right along **The String road** and walk around the rugged slopes at the foot of **Creag Mhor**, passing the access tracks for the farms of **Glaister** and **Monyquil**. Immediately after crossing Glenloig Bridge at the foot of Glen Craigag the circuit is brought to a close back at the small car park at **Glenloig**.

THE STRING

The String road, or B880, cuts the Isle of Arran in half. To the north are high, jagged, rocky mountain peaks, surrounded by a tall deer fence. To the south are lower hills, extensive moorlands and forests. The String road was surveyed by Thomas Telford in 1817, though traces of earlier paths and tracks can still be distinguished on parallel courses on the adjacent slopes.

WALK 22
Blackwaterfoot and King's Cave

Distance	10km (6 miles)
Height gain	100m/330ft
Start/finish	Blackwaterfoot Harbour – grid ref. 895282
Terrain	Clear paths, tracks and roads, but some of the paths can be wet and muddy.
Refreshments	Hotels at Blackwaterfoot have bars and restaurants, and there is also a tearoom at the nearby golf course.

One of the most popular easy walks on the Isle of Arran heads for the King's Cave. There are two paths allowing easy approaches: one from Blackwaterfoot and the other from Machrie Moor. These paths can be combined so that a route from Blackwaterfoot to the King's Cave and onwards to Machrie Moor is possible. Both ends of the walk have car parks (the route may also be started at the car park at the northern end of the route – follow the text from Machrie Moor) and bus services, but the only easy way to turn the walk into a circuit involves following the road back to Blackwaterfoot. Paths shown on maps of Machrie Moor are quite overgrown and difficult to follow, and so are not particularly recommended. Before setting off, walkers should note that there is a gate across the mouth of the King's Cave, protecting the cave from vandalism and misuse, and this may be open or it may be locked. Anyone who wants to explore deep inside the cave may need to obtain a key in advance.

Start from the car park beside the Kinloch Hotel in **Blackwaterfoot** and follow the main road across the bridge overlooking the tiny **harbour**. On the other side of the bridge is a little waterfall. Continue along the main coastal road, then switch to a minor road signposted on the left for a golf course. This road reaches a private car park for the **Shiskine Golf and Tennis Club** and the

Blackwaterfoot Bowling Club. There is a public footpath sign indicating the way to the King's Cave.

Follow a broad coastal track, noting a couple of rocky dykes standing above the level of the **sandy beach**. Low sand dunes are covered in spiky marram grass. The track turns inland and reaches the piers of a **gateway** in a fence. Turn left at this point, where there is another sign for the King's Cave. Follow the fence until signs indicate a way up to another **gate**. A path crosses two fields before a **waymark post** points to the left, revealing a path zigzagging down onto a raised beach.

Note the columnar cliffs facing the sea at **Doon**, draped in ivy and covered in plants and flowers safe from grazing sheep. (There is an option to turn left and follow a narrow path for a short way beneath the cliff-line.) The top of the Doon bears traces of an Iron Age hill fort. Turn right to follow a cobbly, grassy path past an old **sea stack** now marooned on the raised beach. The rock is exotically encrusted with lichens. The route proceeds easily on short grass, then climbs as a narrow, **rocky path** to avoid a bouldery beach walk.

A series of caves are encountered; at least fifteen distinct examples. The first cave is small and choked with brambles. The second is larger, while the third and fourth are separated only by a pillar of rock. There is plenty of headroom for those who want to walk from one to the other. The fifth cave is narrower and is like a passageway leading through to the entrance to the **King's Cave**, which is itself the sixth in the series.

The columnar cliffs of The Doon are seen on the way to the King's Cave

KING'S CAVE

History and mystery surround the caves between Blackwaterfoot and Machrie. There are some interesting carvings from the early Christian and Pictish periods, and the caves are thought to have been used by early Christian voyagers and missionaries to the islands. Some legends state that Robert the Bruce hid in the King's Cave (hence the name) and had his renowned encounter with the spider, or waited for a signal beacon to be lit, but there is no evidence to support either tale. It is, however, quite possible that he used the cave briefly while fleeing to Rathlin Island off the Antrim coast of Northern Ireland in 1306.

A sign fixed to a decorative set of railings reads: 'It has been necessary to restrict access to the cave in order to preserve this important archaeological site which has evidence of human occupation dating back thousands of years. Interested parties can still gain access to the cave. For further information please telephone the Tourist Information Centre at Brodick on 01770 302140.'

The seventh cave is a narrow slit, found just beyond the entrance to the **King's Cave,** which can be walked through. The eighth cave is choked with scrub and the ninth is just beyond a short drystone wall. The 10th cave is a step up above the raised beach, while the 11th is quite low-cut. The 12th is almost obscured by boulders and it is possible to crawl beneath a low arch to reach the 13th. Only consider crawling if you are wearing old clothes, as the floor of the cave is quite mucky. The 14th cave is wet and muddy, while the 15th has a pool of water inside.

The path climbs uphill immediately beside the 15th cave. It rises from a **pebbly beach** and can be muddy until it passes through a gate and proceeds through a **rocky cutting**. A clear, broad, earth and stone path runs uphill parallel to the edge of a forest on the slopes of **Torr Righ Mòr**. It runs along the edge of a heathery brow overlooking the sea and the distant hills of Kintyre. The path climbs over a rise offering views over the gentle farming landscape of **Machrie**. It then runs gently downhill to cross a burn, then climbs a little inside the forest before passing a **hut circle** and dropping to a car park. ▶

The **car park** could be used as an alternative starting point, and it is signposted in advance whichever way you approach it by road. While maps may show paths on nearby **Machrie Moor**, and the Machrie Moor Stone Circles look deceptively close on the map, there is no easy way to tie everything together in a circular walk. Machrie Moor is rough and boggy and the few paths that cross it are quite overgrown and difficult to follow.

An **information board** beside the car park indicates the location of more ancient hut circles nearby, as well as offering notes about the King's Cave and the Machrie Moor Stone Circles.

MACHRIE MOOR

The farming landscape of Machrie Moor has a very long history. Hut circles are dotted all over the slopes of Torr Righ Mòr. A series of famous stone circles, standing stones and burial cairns are located nearby. The hut circles date from Late Neolithic to Early Bronze Age. The stone circles on Machrie Moor are reckoned to be around 4000 years old. The existence of these remains and monuments indicates that a series of settled, agricultural communities lived in this area, which may have been the most fertile and productive area on the Isle of Arran. Walk 23 visits the Machrie Moor Stone Circles.

To return to Blackwaterfoot, the **main road** is all that is available. Turn right to follow it after leaving the forest car park. The road overlooks **Machrie Moor** and is often flanked by shrubs and scrub. A small sign later announces the scattered settlement of **Torbeg**. Shiskine Free Church of Scotland church stands to the right, while to the left at a road junction is a **memorial** to a former minister, the Rev. Archibald Nichol. The main road continues straight on towards Blackwaterfoot, climbing uphill and passing a **small school**, then running gradually downhill, passing the Greannan Bed and Breakfast and a number of bungalows. Turn left at the bottom to follow the coastal road into **Blackwaterfoot**. Most of the facilities in the village are concentrated on either sides of the tiny harbour.

BLACKWATERFOOT

Originally Blackwaterfoot was a small, close-knit community with a few houses positioned around the tiny harbour. There was a massive burial cairn above the village, but this was gradually reduced and plundered for building material. In 1900 a bronze dagger with gold decoration was retrieved from the centre of the cairn.

Facilities from north to south through the village include: Greannan Bed and Breakfast, golf course and tearoom, the Harbour Shop and butcher. On the other side of the bridge and tiny harbour are toilets, a car park and the large Best Western Kinloch Hotel. Continuing uphill comes the Salon, Morvern Guest House, post office and grocery (with ATM), and cycle hire. The Blackwaterfoot Lodge has a bar and restaurant, facing a garage and the Cairnhouse Farm Bed and Breakfast. On the way out of the village, the Cairnhouse Riding Centre is passed.

WALK 23
Machrie Moor Stone Circles

Distance	3km (2 miles)
Height gain	40m/130ft
Start/finish	Near Machrie Water – grid ref. 895330
Terrain	A good track ending with moorlands that can be wet underfoot.
Refreshments	The Machrie Bay Tearoom is off-route.

One of the easiest and most interesting walks on the Isle of Arran is the one to the Machrie Moor Stone Circles. This could be accomplished in almost any weather, but in fine weather there is a chance to experience the refreshing spaciousness of the site. A number of stone circles and standing stones can be inspected from a gravel track and moorland path. All around are ranged some of the highest and most rugged mountains on the island, which make a superb backdrop for photographers wanting to capture the spirit of the place. The only drawback is that the area can be busy with other visitors, so walking there in the quiet times of the year can be a good idea.

This short, easy walk starts beside the main road near **Machrie Water**. There is a sign beside the road reading 'Machrie Moor Stone Circles 1 mile', and there is a small car park available. Leave the road at a **gate and stile** and follow a clear and obvious track across fields. The track rises and bends right and left. At another gate and stile the **Moss Farm Road Stone Circle** stands in a fenced enclosure and can be inspected.

The track continues clearly over a moorland rise, and there are **small standing stones** to right and left. Shortly afterwards, pass through a gateway to find a **stone circle** to the right, above the derelict buildings of **Moss Farm**. Cross a nearby stile and study information boards relating to **Machrie Moor**.

There is a **stone circle** to the right of the information boards, and a narrow moorland path leads to **three tall standing stones**. Beyond these are two more **stone circles**. Retracing steps a little, but branching off to the right, is a tall, **solitary standing stone**. All around this moorland setting are ranged the peaks of Beinn Bharrain, Sail Chalmadale, Beinn Nuis, Goat Fell and Ard Bheinn. When all the stone circles and standing stones have been thoroughly investigated, simply retrace steps from **Moss Farm** back along the gravel track to return to the small car park beside the main road. If you arrived by bus and have time to spare before the next one arrives, then head for the nearby golf course and **Machrie Bay Tearoom**.

MACHRIE MOOR STONE CIRCLES

Machrie Moor is a well-preserved Neolithic and Bronze Age ritual landscape. The Moss Farm Road Stone Circle is unusual as it may actually be a kerbed cairn, or the cairn was constructed before the stone circle. Apart from stone circles and standing stones, the area around Machrie Moor is dotted with hut circles, indicating that people lived in a settled, agricultural community. There must have been a high degree of community involvement for them to have raised so many fine structures and monuments, and this must have been one of the most fertile parts of the Isle of Arran to sustain such a population.

*One of the prominent standing stones
seen on the spacious Machrie Moor*

WALK 24
Dougarie and Beinn Nuis

Distance	22km (13.5 miles), or a short version of 15km (9.5 miles)
Height gain	850m/2790ft
Start/finish	Dougarie – grid ref. 882370
Terrain	Some tracks, but mostly pathless moorlands and mountain, boggy and bouldery in many places. Roads are used at the end.
Refreshments	The Machrie Bay Tearoom is just off-route at Machrie.

Beinn Nuis is almost always climbed from Glen Rosa, and that is the way its paths are trodden. Its rugged form dominates Glen Iorsa, but few walkers attempt a summit bid from that direction and there are very few trodden paths on the way. The route described here uses the access track leading to Loch Iorsa, then heads for the desolate uplands, reaching Beinn Nuis by way of a fine, bouldery ridge. There is an opportunity to walk round the bouldery bowl of Coire Nuis, then head back across empty moorlands to reach Loch Nuis. While steps could be retraced through Glen Iorsa, another ending can be contemplated, following a forest fence across boggy moorland slopes to descend to Machrie. A short road walk leads back from Machrie to Dougarie. There is a shorter alternative route: walkers can climb above Glen Iorsa, then instead of climbing Beinn Nuis, they can simply turn right and follow the forest fence straight across the moorlands to Machrie. Note that when Iorsa Water is in spate it is difficult to complete this walk; for an alternative follow Walk 25.

There are only small spaces to park cars at **Dougarie**, some distance from either side of the bridge spanning Iorsa Water at its confluence with the sea. The white-washed **Dougarie Lodge**, which is seen briefly on both sides of the bridge, is private, and a sign indicates that a footpath is available further along the road, in the Pirnmill direction. Walk along the road and round a

bend, then take a **narrow road** on the right, which is sign-posted as a footpath. The tarmac gives way to a concrete track that continues uphill and bends left. Another sign on the bend indicates the footpath heading straight up a **flight of steps**.

Cross a **stile over a wall** at the top of the slope. The path follows the wall through a field, crossing a **stile over a fence**. Continue through a **small wood** and cross another fence, then follow the path across a slope of bracken. The path dips down to cross a **stile** over another fence, then joins a track. Cross either a concrete ford or a footbridge over the **Allt na h' Airidhe** and keep walking along the track in view of **Iorsa Water**.

The river is broad and bouldery and is the biggest river on the island. It cuts through masses of glacial rubble, whose ill-bedded layers can be seen alongside the track. Go through a gate in a tall **deer fence**, then cross a concrete ford at the foot of **Glen Scaftigill**. When the river is in spate you will get wet feet at this point; a footbridge used to span the river upstream, but has been swept away. The track continues across a slope of tussocky grass, heather and bog myrtle to reach the foot of **Loch Iorsa**, where there is a tiny **boathouse**.

Dougarie Lodge and distant Beinn Bharrain are seen from the coastal road

135

A grassy, wet and boggy track pushes further up into **Glen Iorsa**, running alongside the shore of Loch Iorsa, then continuing beside **Iorsa Water**. Bog myrtle grows amid the grass and heather. Watch carefully to spot shoals of **reddish gravel** where the channel is braided and there is a good chance of fording the river without getting wet feet. However, in times of spate and high water, it may be impossible to continue further, and walkers may prefer to switch to the Sail Chalmadale route instead. See Walk 25 for details.

If **Iorsa Water** can be safely forded, then head straight uphill alongside the **Allt Airidh Mhuirich**, which is full of delightful **waterfalls**.

Avoid areas of bracken at the foot of the burn, and walk through tussocky grass, heather and bog myrtle at a higher level. There are even a few trees tucked into the little gorge drained by the burn. Views open up both ways along the bleak and barren length of Glen Iorsa, then the gradient eases and **Loch Nuis** is suddenly reached. ▶

Turn left to walk away from **Loch Nuis**, heading roughly north-east across a huge, boggy, grass and heather moorland. Keep left of **Coire Nuis** to climb up a **boulder-strewn ridge**. The ground steepens and the rounded ridge features views

Walkers who wish to omit the climb to Beinn Nuis and enjoy a shorter walk should simply turn right and walk away from **Loch Nuis**, heading towards a nearby forest to pick up the route description further below at a **forest fence**.

extending from Kintyre and Antrim to Holy Isle and the Ayrshire coast. The climb up the **rounded ridge** proves relatively easy after the tussocky moors. The ground becomes predominantly bouldery, then rather gritty, before a fine, blocky ridge of granite develops, with good views across Glen Iorsa to the Pirnmill Hills. Cross a **little gap**, then climb up a steep slope of short heather and boulders. After passing a wrinkly little **tor of granite**, a gentler, grassier, less bouldery slope leads to the top of **Beinn Nuis**. The bouldery summit bears a little cairn at 792m and features dramatic views around Glen Rosa.

Turn right to follow a path away from the summit cairn. This path runs down a steep, rocky slope beside a **precipitous cliff**. When a gentle gap is reached, the path heads off towards Glen Rosa, but this route turns right to cross a **gentle rise** of short grass, heather, low outcrops and boulders. The end of this little crest steepens abruptly and falls southwards towards a broad, boggy moorland drained by the Garbh Allt. In clear weather, the lonely moorland pool of Loch Nuis will be in view. There are all sorts of vague paths on the moorlands below, but none of them can be followed for any great distance. Head south-west and aim to reach the course of the **Garbh Allt**, crossing it to walk downstream on the other side. **Loch Nuis** will have passed from sight, but aim instead for the corner of a **forest** seen ahead on a rise of moorland. The grass and heather can be tussocky in places and makes for a rough passage.

The **forest fence** is the key to the long descent from the moors. Turn right to follow the fence uphill across a rise of moorland on **Beinn Tarsuinn**. Loch Nuis comes into view again, with Beinn Nuis well framed beyond. The fence runs downhill a short way, then there is a left turn around a **corner**. Continue following the fence downhill, then cross a more level area with many boggy patches. There is a rise and fall as the hump of **Beinn Chaorach** is passed. The fence descends to cross the **Auchencar Burn**, then rises a little, then descends again. Bracken patches impede progress a little near the hump of **Cnoc a' Choire Mhoir**.

Look out for a **track** just to the right of the forest fence. Pick up this line and follow it then use a **ladder stile** to cross a tall deer fence. The grassy track can be traced across fields, crossing the gentle slopes of **Cnocan Cuallaich**. The track runs down towards a huddle of farm buildings at **Auchagallon**. Turn left through a gate and follow the clearest, broadest gravel track, which zigzags downhill. The lowest zigzag turns around a small enclosure where the **Auchagallon Stone Circle** is located.

Continue down to the **road**. This is a minor road, with the main coastal road lying just beyond. Turn right along both roads, walking from the **Machrie Garage** back towards Dougarie. (There is of course the opportunity to walk the other way along the coastal road to take a break at the Machrie Bay Tearoom at a nearby golf course.) A

AUCHAGALLON STONE CIRCLE

Although often referred to as a stone circle, the site at Auchagallon is actually a kerbed cairn. The remaining upright slabs lie inwards around an ancient grassy cairn, probably dating back 4000 years. Excavations carried out in the 19th century revealed a cist burial in the middle of the cairn. Kerbed cairns are thought to have been constructed as burial places for important people, creating a site which would impress visitors and remind them of the importance of the person within. The nearby Moss Farm Road Stone Circle on Machrie Moor, passed on Walk 23, may be of the same type of construction.

scrub-covered sandstone cliff along the way features a handful of caves and a small burial ground. Next comes **The Schoolhouse**, a fine red sandstone building flanked by trees. A signposted turning further along the road offers an optional short detour up to the **Auchencar Druid Stone** and the **Old Byre Showroom**.

AUCHENCAR DRUID STONE

Situated in a large field off the access road for Auchencar, the Druid Stone is the tallest standing stone on the Isle of Arran. The stone itself is a blade of rock, which looks tall and broad from one side, yet tall and narrow from the other. Its isolation in a broad field removed from habitation, yet within view of the mountains, adds to its impressiveness. The broken remains of a similar stone lie embedded in the grass alongside.

OLD BYRE SHOWROOM

The Old Byre Showroom is signposted from the main road, and in this remote setting it is an unlikely place to go shopping for sheepskins, leather goods, woollens and other items of clothing, some with designer labels.

Walkers simply continue along the main coastal road, or switch to follow a pleasant **grassy strip** beside the road, on the final stretch back to **Dougarie**.

WALK 25
Dougarie and Sail Chalmadale

Distance	16 km (10 miles)
Height gain	510m/1675ft
Start/finish	Dougarie – grid ref. 882370
Terrain	Gravel and boggy tracks, as well as pathless uplands, boggy and rocky ground.
Refreshments	None closer than the Machrie Bay Tearoom.

When the high mountains around Glen Iorsa are shrouded in cloud, it is often the case that Sail Chalmadale will be clear. A combination of its lower height and its proximity to loftier neighbours gives it some measure of protection from inclement weather, but a traverse would require careful navigation in mist. The access track running to Loch Iorsa from Dougarie is an obvious way towards Sail Chalmadale, and the mountain can be climbed gradually in a sort of spiral route from the glen. A descent can be made back towards the main track in the glen, finishing with a walk back to the main road at Dougarie. Despite its low stature, Sail Chalmadale offers a fine, rugged upland walk.

There are only small spaces to park cars at **Dougarie**, some distance from either side of the bridge spanning Iorsa Water at its confluence with the sea. The whitewashed **Dougarie Lodge**, which is seen briefly on both sides of the bridge, is private, and a sign indicates that a footpath is available further along the road, in the Pirnmill direction. Walk along the road and round a bend, then take a **narrow road** on the right, which is signposted as a footpath. The tarmac gives way to a concrete track that continues uphill and bends left. Another sign on the bend indicates the footpath heading straight up a **flight of steps**.

Cross a **stile over a wall** at the top of the slope. The path follows the wall through a field, crossing a **stile over a fence**. Continue through a **small wood** and cross another fence, then follow the path across a slope of bracken. The path dips down to cross a **stile** over another fence, then joins a track. Cross either a concrete ford or a footbridge over the **Allt na h' Airidhe** and keep walking along the track in view of **Iorsa Water**.

The river is broad and bouldery and is the biggest river on the island. It cuts through masses of glacial rubble, whose ill-bedded layers can be seen alongside the track. Go through a gate in a tall deer fence, then cross a concrete ford at the foot of Glen Scaftigill.

When the river is in spate, you will get wet feet at this point; a footbridge used to span the river upstream, but has been swept away. The track continues across a slope of tussocky grass,

A small boathouse stands beside Loch Iorsa deep within the remote Glen Iorsa

heather and bog myrtle to reach the foot of Loch Iorsa, where there is a tiny boathouse.

A grassy, wet and boggy track pushes further up into **Glen Iorsa**, running alongside the shore of Loch Iorsa, then continuing beside **Iorsa Water**. Bog myrtle grows amid the grass and heather. The track has been blazed by quad bikes being ridden into the glen and is braided in places. The route avoids the broad and boggy floor of the glen, and sticks instead to the lower slopes of Sail Chalmadale. Follow this track as far as the **Allt Tigh an Shiorraim**, crossing both channels of the bouldery burn. Turn left to trace the burn upstream, but also keep well to the right of it for easier walking.

Aim to walk along the top of a **high bank** overlooking the bouldery watercourse, where a vague path can be traced through the grass and heather, weaving past scattered boulders. At a higher level all traces of the path are lost, but it is still a good idea to keep to a rugged **moorland shelf** above the burn. Later, choose any point at which to **ford** the burn, even to the extent of going all the way up to **Loch Tanna** to enjoy a close-up view of Arran's largest lake. Obviously, the higher the burn is forded, the less climbing there is on the slope opposite.

Walk roughly southwards along a broad and rugged crest. This is bouldery, with grass and heather, as well as exposed gritty soil in places. Walk along the crest, passing well to the left side of the little **Lochan nan**

Cnamh. Walk up a slope of rocky ribs and low boulders, crossing the rugged, domed summit of **Cnoc Breac** at 428m. Cross over a little gap, then climb another bouldery slope at a fairly gentle gradient. There is a cairn on top of **Sail Chalmadale** at 480m, surrounded by boulders poking up from short heather. ▶

There is a **narrow path** trodden away from the summit, running roughly southwards, but it soon vanishes. Keep walking onwards until the lower parts of the ridge can be seen, bearing two small lochans. Start to drift to the left to descend more steeply, avoiding unseen **sloping slabs** of granite. Swing back to the right later, and keep well to the right of the **two lochans**, which pass from sight until they are approached more closely on the broad moorland shoulder. Vague paths will be spotted in this direction, and it should be possible to trace them further downhill. The lower slopes, around **Creag a' Chromain**, are largely of tussocky grass, heather, bracken and bog myrtle.

When the main **track** running through Glen Iorsa is gained, it is simply a matter of turning right and retracing the earlier steps of the day. Cross the concrete ford at the foot of **Glen Scaftigill** and pass through the gate in the tall **deer fence**. Follow the track to the next ford and **footbridge**. A small sign indicates the **footpath** to the road off to the right. Cross the slope of bracken, walk through the **small wood** and two fields, then go down the **steps** and follow the track back to the main coastal road at **Dougarie**.

The view includes a host of higher summits arranged around Glen Iorsa. Looking seawards, it is possible to spot Jura, Kintyre, Antrim and even Ailsa Craig over a shoulder of broad moorland.

DOUGARIE LODGE

The attractive Dougarie Lodge was built towards the end of the 19th century as a shooting lodge. Although the red deer population on Arran had almost been wiped out by the beginning of the 19th century, there was considerable restocking and the northern half of the island was made into a deer forest secured by a tall deer fence. At one time the exterior of Dougarie Lodge was covered in antlers, but now the building is simply whitewashed. There is no access to the lodge, and walkers are directed along a footpath that keeps well away from the building.

WALK 26
Circuit of Glen Iorsa

Distance	32km (20 miles)
Height gain	1850m/6070ft
Start/finish	Dougarie – grid ref. 882370
Terrain	Some good ridge paths and vague moorland paths, but often rocky, boggy terrain.
Refreshments	None closer than the Machrie Bay Tearoom.

One of the toughest and most remote day's walks on the Isle of Arran must be the circuit around Glen Iorsa. This broad, bleak and boggy glen slices through northern Arran and is without any habitations apart from Dougarie Lodge beside the sea. The route takes in Sail Chalmadale, Loch Tanna, Beinn Tarsuinn and Loch na Davie. There are ascents of Caisteal Abhail and the rocky Cir Mhòr. By-passing the rocky ridge of A' Chir, the route climbs over Beinn Tarsuinn and Beinn Nuis before making a long descent towards Loch Iorsa. Paths are few and vague for the first half of the walk, though they are much clearer over the higher, rockier mountains. Walkers who attempt this long and hard walk should have an escape plan in mind. While a descent into Glen Iorsa is possible from many points, it could involve crossing very rugged, pathless terrain. Descents into other glens might be preferable.

There are only small spaces to park cars at **Dougarie**, some distance from either side of the bridge spanning Iorsa Water at its confluence with the sea. The white-washed **Dougarie Lodge**, which is seen briefly on both sides of the bridge, is private, and a sign indicates that a footpath is available further along the road, in the Pirnmill direction. Walk along the road and round a bend, then take a **narrow road** on the right, which is sign-posted as a footpath. The tarmac gives way to a concrete track that continues uphill and bends left. Another sign on the bend indicates the footpath heading straight up a **flight of steps**.

Cross a stile over a wall at the top of the slope. The path follows the wall through a field, crossing a stile over a fence. Continue through a small wood and cross another fence, then follow the path across a slope of bracken. The path dips down to cross a stile over another fence, then joins a track. Cross either a concrete ford or a footbridge over the **Allt na h' Airidhe** and keep walking along the track in view of **Iorsa Water**.

The river is broad and bouldery and is the biggest river on the island. It cuts through masses of glacial rubble, whose ill-bedded layers can be seen alongside the track. Go through a gate in a tall **deer fence**, then cross a concrete ford at the foot of **Glen Scaftigill**. When the river is in spate, you will get wet feet at this point; a footbridge used to span the river upstream, but has been swept away.

Turn left to leave the track and pick up any vague paths climbing up the lower slopes of Sail Chalmadale. Cross tussocky grass, heather, bracken and bog myrtle on the way up past **Creag a' Chromain**, then pass to the left of **two lochans** on a moorland shoulder. The rugged hill rises ahead, but there are **sloping slabs** of granite in view.

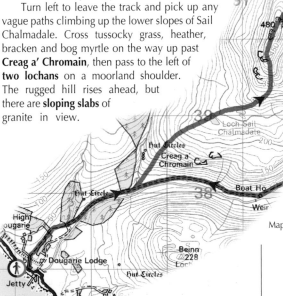

Map continues p.146

Keep well to the right to outflank these and climb more steeply uphill. The higher crest is much gentler and there is even a vague path leading across short heather and boulders to the summit cairn on **Sail Chalmadale** at 480m. There is a chance to observe the whole of the route around Glen Iorsa, stretching from Loch Tanna to Caisteal Abhail and Beinn Nuis. It is a daunting prospect after the rather tough ascent of lowly Sail Chalmadale.

Continue walking along the crest of the hill, heading down a bouldery slope to cross a little gap. Walk over the rugged, domed summit of **Cnoc Breac**, at 428m, and cross rocky ribs and boulders on the short descent towards **Lochan nan Cnamh**. Pass the lochan on its right side and continue across a broad moorland slope which is bouldery in some parts and clothed in tussocky grass and heather in other parts. Aim for the outflow from **Loch Tanna**, fording the **Allt Tigh an Shiorraim** to walk along the eastern shore of the loch. This is the largest lake on the Isle of Arran, and the most remote.

Following the shore of the loch is rather too rough and wet, so it is better to drift away from the shore and head northwards towards the hills. The moorland slope can be boggy and rocky in places, and as the ground steepens there is prostrate juniper couched amid the rock and heather. The first part of **Beinn Tarsuinn** is broad, gritty, bouldery and features some low outcrops of granite. The only **cairn** is a small construction just off the 527m summit. Continue across the summit, down to a broad, boggy gap, then climb uphill towards a slightly higher part of Beinn Tarsuinn. Don't go to the 556m summit, but drift to the right and drop gently onto a **bouldery shoulder**. Next, bear left and make a steep and bouldery descent from the crest of Beinn Tarsuinn to a **broad gap** of boggy ground and stony patches over 400m.

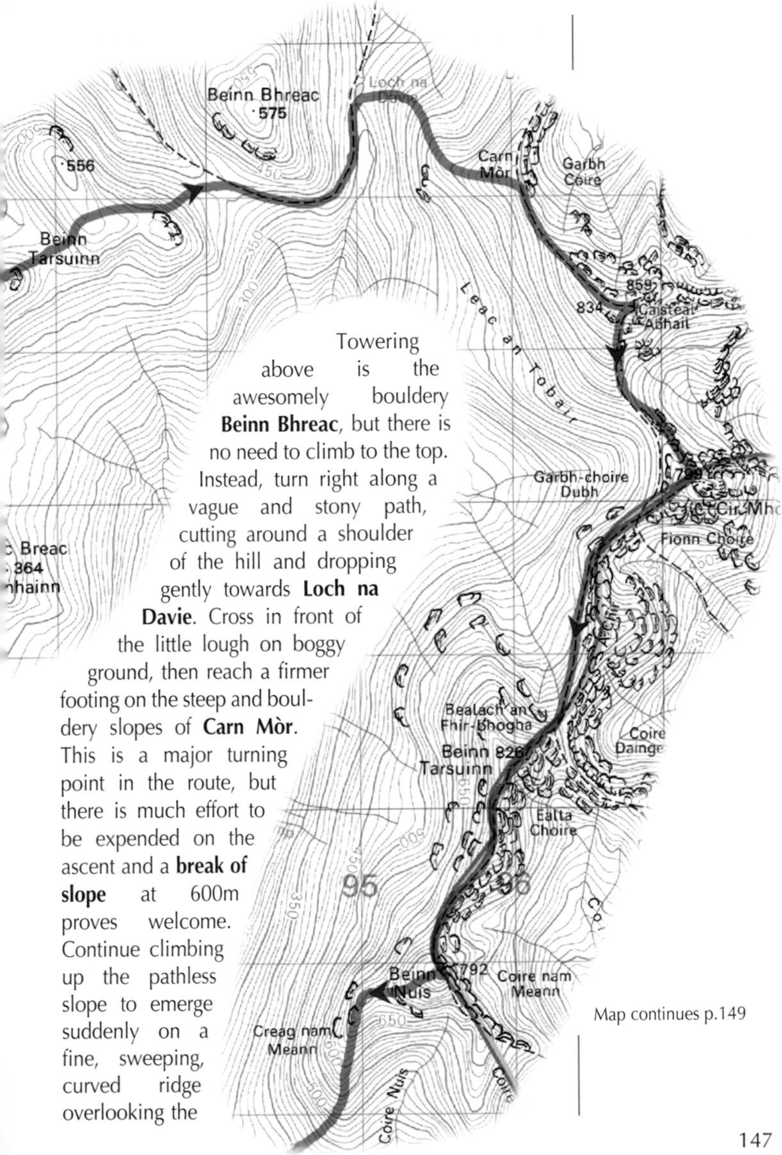

Beinn Bhreac
·575

·556

Loch na

Carn
Mòr

Garbh
Coire

Beinn
Tarsuinn

Leac an Tobair

859
834
Caisteal
Abhail

: Breac
·364
nhainn

Garbh-choire
Dubh

Cir Mhòr

Fionn Choire

Towering above is the awesomely bouldery **Beinn Bhreac**, but there is no need to climb to the top. Instead, turn right along a vague and stony path, cutting around a shoulder of the hill and dropping gently towards **Loch na Davie**. Cross in front of the little lough on boggy ground, then reach a firmer footing on the steep and bouldery slopes of **Carn Mòr**. This is a major turning point in the route, but there is much effort to be expended on the ascent and a **break of slope** at 600m proves welcome. Continue climbing up the pathless slope to emerge suddenly on a fine, sweeping, curved ridge overlooking the

Bealach an
Fhir-Bhogha

Beinn 826
Tarsuinn

Coire
Daing...

Ealta
Choire

95

96

Beinn
Nuis

792

Coire nam
Meann

Creag nam
Meann

Map continues p.149

Coire Nuis

This ridge is often referred to as the 'dress circle'.

Garbh Choire. ◄ A right turn up the ridge leads eventually to the summit of **Caisteal Abhail** at 859m. There are a handful of **granite tors** on the summit which have the appearance of ruined castles.

Pick a way roughly southwards down from the summit and walk around the rough and rocky **Coire nan Uamh**. The next summit in line is the impressively steep and rocky pyramid of **Cir Mhòr**. Walkers should feel drawn to climb all the way to the 799m summit, but the walk is already well advanced and some may be having problems. Dissipating energy and dwindling daylight are to be guarded against, and it is only fair to point out that there is a **path** cutting across the Glen Iorsa flank of Cir Mhòr, omitting the rocky summit.

Rising above the next gap are the rocky buttresses of **A' Chir**, where walkers would normally not tread. The full traverse of the A' Chir ridge is technically a rock climb, with some very exposed moves. Walkers start by climbing along the rocky crest, but should look carefully for a **path** ducking off to the right, from some flat slabs on the Glen Iorsa flank of the mountain. This narrow, stony, rocky path sneaks across a rugged slope and passes beneath weeping **boilerplate slabs** of granite which support only a few little rugs of heather. The path then climbs gradually to the next gap, which is **Bealach an Fhir-bhogha**.

Towering above Bealach an Fhir-bhogha are dark granite buttresses, which frown on humble walkers – especially those who are tired and still have a long walk ahead of them. A rocky, bouldery path keeps to the right of the **main buttress**, and although there are sometimes alternative lines available, all of them involve the use of hands for balance at some point. The lower parts are tougher than the upper parts, and there is even the option of walking beneath a **huge boulder** at one point. There are twin summits on **Beinn Tarsuinn** at 826m; both have low outcrops and boulders of granite. A short, bouldery slope leads down to a dip and on the short pull upwards the human profile of the **Old Man of Tarsuinn** will be seen to the left. A narrow ridge runs downhill, broadens and becomes covered in moss and short grass. Large rounded boulders are passed as the ridge broadens, then a **narrow gap** is crossed before a short ascent of a steep and bouldery slope leads onto the top of **Beinn Nuis**. A small cairn sits on the summit at 792m.

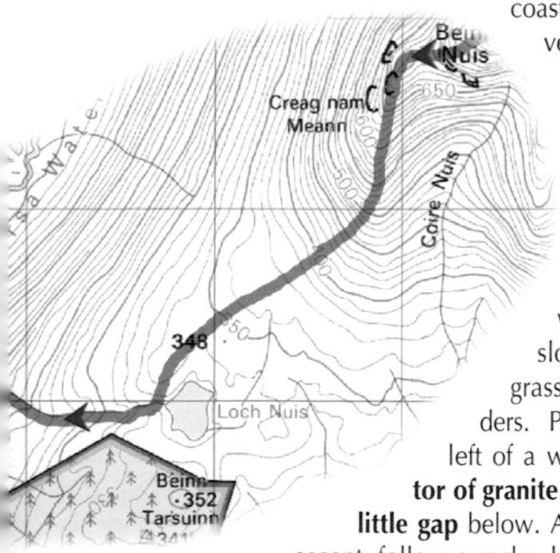

Views extend along the length of Glen Iorsa from this final summit, but the coast still seems very distant. Walk westwards to leave, quickly swinging more south-west on a slope of short grass and boulders. Pass to the left of a wrinkly little **tor of granite** and cross a **little gap** below. After a short ascent, follow a rocky, blocky ridge downhill. The ridge broadens and becomes gritty, then more bouldery and heathery. Below the **rounded ridge** is

The view from Beian Nuis before the long descent and walk-out to Dougarie

an expanse of moorland broken by the shape of Loch Nuis. Head off to the right of the ridge, and cross a moorland rise, keeping to the right of **Loch Nuis**. A couple of rashes of boulders are passed on the moorland, and the **Allt Airidh Mhuirich** can be forded quite easily near the loch.

Walk downstream beside the Allt Airidh Mhuirich and enjoy the sight of its little **waterfalls**. Drift away to the left before it joins **Iorsa Water**, and look carefully to spot shoals of **reddish gravel** in the river, where the channel is braided and shallow, so that you should normally be able to find a way across without getting wet feet. ◀ Once across the river, turn left and pick up the course of a boggy, **grassy track** made by quad bikes, and follow this roughly parallel to **Loch Iorsa**. At the foot of Loch Iorsa is a tiny **boathouse** and a gravel track.

*Bear in mind that the river could be too **dangerous to cross after heavy rain**, in which case you should refer to Walk 24 and make an exit from Loch Nuis to Machrie alongside a forest fence.*

The gravel track marks firm ground and a safe exit after the endless mountains and bogs of this circuit. Follow the track down through **Glen Iorsa** to reach the concrete ford at the foot of **Glen Scaftigill** and pass through the gate in the tall **deer fence**. Follow the track to the next ford and **footbridge**. A small sign indicates the **footpath** to the road off to the right. Cross the slope of bracken, walk through the **small wood** and two fields, then go down the **steps** and follow the track back to the main coastal road at **Dougarie**.

WALK 27
Imachar and Beinn Bharrain

Distance	19km (12 miles)
Height gain	890m/2920ft
Start/finish	Between Whitefarland and Imachar – grid ref. 863413
Terrain	Forest tracks and mountain paths, but mostly pathless moorland needing care in mist.
Refreshments	None closer than the Lighthouse café at Pirnmill.

A large forest plantation has been established on Ceann Reamhar and Roileag above Whitefarland and Imachar. While not being particularly lovely, it is largely tucked out of sight. It is served by clear gravel tracks that run fairly close to Beinn Bharrain. These forest tracks are used on the outward and return journeys, and the plan is to link them with a high-level walk over the top of Beinn Bharrain (sometimes referred to as Mullach Buidhe). Bear in mind that rugged and largely pathless slopes surround the mountain. The route has been structured to include the lonely Dubh Loch and Loch Tanna, as well as the unfrequented head of Glen Scaftigill. As some parts are quite rugged, this is a walk for the agile, sure-footed walker who can navigate competently in mist.

Start on the main coastal road between the farmsteads at **Imachar** and **Whitefarland**. There is a track running uphill from the road, flanked by **double gates**. Parking is not possible at this point, or for some distance either way along the road, but walkers using bus services can simply hop off at this point and start walking. The **track** climbs across a hillside that is variously vegetated, but mostly covered in grass and bracken. The track zigzags right and left, passing a prominent **mast** in a small compound beside two brick huts. Continue along the track, passing through a gate, then reaching a taller gate in a **deer fence** surrounding a forest. There is much more heather evident at this point.

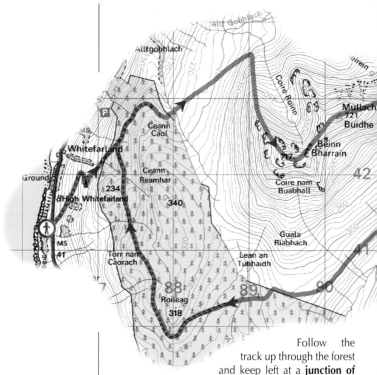

Follow the track up through the forest and keep left at a **junction of tracks**. The track follows a broad, heathery strip through the forest, then bends sharply to the right as it continues to climb. It expires suddenly on a broad, **heathery ride**. Turn left and follow another short ride downhill to the **forest fence**. There is no gate, though there is evidence that other people have walked this way. Very thin walkers could squeeze beneath the tall deer fence, while more portly ones could climb at a straining post. Either way, agility is called for and this should be borne in mind before starting the walk.

Head straight towards a **burn** in a rocky cut outside the forest. Look carefully and a rather narrow, precarious **path** will be spotted crossing from one side to the other.

Pick a way across with care, but note that it may be impassable when swollen with floodwater. Walk across a broad **moorland** slope, keeping well to the left of the huge mountain ahead. Aim to avoid the steep, bouldery slopes and instead join the ridge to the left. There is a **path** running all the way up the ridge at a less severe gradient than a direct summit bid. The path climbs and crosses **granite slabs** at first, where it is necessary to look carefully for its continuation at times. Heather on the steep path later gives way to short grass, though the **rounded ridge** is scattered with boulders throughout the ascent. At the top there is a **small tor** of tilted granite blocks, then the path is more vague as it crosses the broad summit. There is a **cairn** at 717m marking the highest part of the mountain.

Walk across the short grass, passing low outcrops and boulders. Climb onto what appears to be a little **tor**, noting that there is a considerable gap on the far side. The steep and rocky slope bears a zigzag path leading down past granite slabs to a **gap**. The path climbs uphill from the gap, and its narrow line can be traced past a couple of **blocky tors** to reach the summit of **Beinn Bharrain** at 721m. There is a cairn and a trig point, with extensive views in clear weather.

Look carefully for the path leaving the summit, picking a way roughly east and north-east down a **rounded ridge** of scoured, gritty soil and short grass. The slope becomes less steep, but also more bouldery and narrow. The lowest part of the ridge is **Bealach an Fharaidh**, where care should be taken to spot a path heading off to the right. Drop steeply downhill on a rather worn and **stony path**. Anyone wanting to avoid this route could walk on the rough, bouldery slopes to

Dubh Loch and Loch Tanna are seen on the moorlands below Beinn Bharrain

either side. When the slope begins to level out, masses of prostrate juniper can be seen amid the boulders and heather. Head directly across a rugged, boggy moorland slope, passing the outflow of little **Dubh Loch** on the way to the foot of **Loch Tanna**. This is the largest lake on the Isle of Arran, and also the most remote.

Head roughly south-west from the foot of Loch Tanna. The idea is to climb very gently across a rugged, boggy moorland to reach a **broad gap** between Beinn Bharrain and Sail Chalmadale. Cross this gap and descend into the head of **Glen Scaftigill**. The walking is fairly easy, though there is no trodden path at all. Cross grass, heather and bog myrtle on the gradual drift down towards the **burn** draining the glen. This is a bouldery, rocky burn and there are plenty of places where it can be crossed. After crossing, the ground on the far side is rather more rough and tussocky. Climb very gradually across the slopes of the glen, roughly contouring around 250m, to reach the edge of a **coniferous plantation** seen straight ahead. A tall deer fence surrounds the forest and there is a sort of trodden path alongside it.

Turn right to follow the **deer fence** over the top of a broad and boggy rise. As it starts to descend, there is a **gate** on the left. Go through the gate and follow a **ride** into the forest for a short way. Turn right to walk down a grassy, mossy **track** through a wide, grassy, heathery strip between the trees. Cross a **burn** and join a clear **gravel track** at the same time. Follow the track uphill on a broad, heathery ride. The track bends well to the right at the top of the rise at **Roileag**, and there are some views across Kilbrannan Sound to Kintyre.

The track descends very gradually across the forested slopes of Roileag and **Ceann Reamhar**, crossing some unplanted swathes of moorland. When a **junction** of gravel tracks is reached, note that this point was passed earlier in the day. Turn left to continue downhill, passing both the **tall gate** at the edge of the forest, and the next gate, before the track zigzags downhill past the **mast**. Simply continue downhill across the grass and bracken slope to end back on the road between **Imachar** and **Whitefarland**.

A view of Beinn Bharrain from the burn that is forded inside the forest plantation

WALK 28
Pirnmill and Beinn Bharrain

Distance	13km (8 miles)
Height gain	940m/3085ft
Start/finish	The Lighthouse café, Pirnmill – grid ref. 872441
Terrain	Rugged hillwalking, mostly on good paths, but some areas have no paths.
Refreshments	The Lighthouse café, Pirnmill.

Beinn Bharrain, sometimes referred to as Mullach Buidhe, is the highest of the Pirnmill Hills grouped in the north-west of the Isle of Arran. It rises steeply above the straggly little village of Pirnmill. The village makes a handy starting point for the walk and there is good access to a rugged moorland shelf. Paths are vague across the moorland shelf, though there is a fairly well trodden path along the mountain ridge high above. It is worth climbing Beinn Bhreac as well as Beinn Bharrain in order to make the most of the high ridge, although the ascent to the ridge by way of Meall Donn is steep and unremitting. In clear weather, views from the ridge are remarkably extensive and take in all the highest peaks on the Isle of Arran.

Start at the Lighthouse café in **Pirnmill**, beside the village store. Face the café, noting that there is a clear **gravel track** off to the left, running straight uphill from its junction with the main coastal road. The track swings to the left, then turns right and runs uphill. When the track bends to the left, don't follow it, but look carefully off to the right to spot a **stile** over a fence. A narrow and muddy **path** squeezes between densely planted young trees, but a more open stand of oak is encountered at a higher level. There are views between the oak and birch trees over some fine, slender **waterfalls** deep within a gorge. Follow the path further uphill, crossing a couple of small **stiles** alongside a deer fence, then cross a large

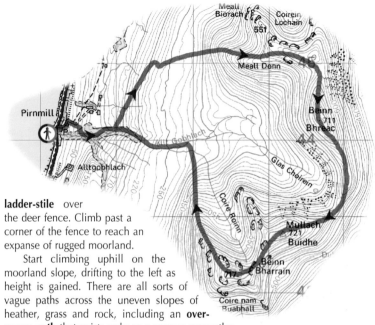

ladder-stile over
the deer fence. Climb past a
corner of the fence to reach an
expanse of rugged moorland.

Start climbing uphill on the
moorland slope, drifting to the left as
height is gained. There are all sorts of
vague paths across the uneven slopes of
heather, grass and rock, including an **overgrown path** that exists only as a groove across the
moor. If this feature is discovered, then follow it, otherwise simply make a bee-line towards Meall Donn,
crossing a gentler slope of more boggy ground on the
way. The steep slopes of **Meall Donn** are covered in
heather and boulders, without any clear paths. Choose
any route uphill, noting that the ground is less bouldery
further to the left. The steep slope is unremitting, but
taken steadily there is an eventual **break of slope** where
the walking becomes easier. Follow the rounded,
heathery, bouldery crest onwards and upwards. A path is
eventually gained on another broad crest overlooking
Fion Lochan. Turn right and follow this gently uphill to a
broad and bouldery summit at 653m.

Continue straight along the rounded, bouldery crest,
using a **path** that proves to be quite easy despite the
boulders. The path leads to a large summit cairn on

Beinn Bhreac and Beinn Bharrain rise as rugged domes from the broad ridge

Beinn Bhreac at 711m. There is a sudden view straight ahead stretching beyond the Isle of Arran to the prominent pyramid of Ailsa Craig. Leave the summit and continue along the rounded, bouldery ridge, following a **path** that is rather vague in places. The ridge levels out on a shoulder, then there are larger boulders to be crossed on the way down to the gap of **Bealach an Fharaidh**. Climb uphill from the gap, stepping across some large boulders at first. The slope becomes less bouldery, but rather steeper too, featuring scoured gritty soil and short grass. The top of **Beinn Bharrain** is fairly broad, bearing a cairn and trig point at 721m.

Walk along the broad crest, walking on short grass, following a vague path and passing a couple of blocky little **granite tors**. The path remains narrow, but is more clearly trodden down to the next **gap**. A steep slope ahead bears a zigzag path, which passes **granite slabs** on the rockier parts of a prominent **tor**. The top of this tor is a prominent summit in its own right, and this should be borne in mind in poor visibility. Drop down slightly from the tor and follow the **path** further across the broad summit, walking on short grass and passing low outcrops and boulders. There is a **cairn** at 717m on the highest part of the mountain.

Walk across the broad summit, drifting to the right towards a **small tor** of tilted granite blocks. A path leaves the tor, running straight down a **rounded ridge** scattered with boulders. Later, the ground steepens and short grass gives way to heather. Look carefully for the line of the path after it runs onto **granite slabs** then follow it down onto a gentler sloping, but more rugged moorland, which can be boggy underfoot. Only a vague path crosses the lower moorland, so be sure to swing to the right to cross a river, the **Allt Gobhlach**, well before it plunges into a steep, wooded gorge. Stay clear of the **gorge** on the final stage of the descent, enjoying views of its **waterfalls**, aiming to reach the corner of the deer fence that was crossed earlier in the day's walk. Cross the **ladder stile** over the deer fence, then follow the narrow path down-hill alongside the fence. Cross two smaller **stiles** as the path runs down through a birch and oak woodland, looking into the gorge to spot more fine waterfalls. The **path** has a muddy stretch before a **stile** gives way to a firm **track**. Turn left and follow the track back down to **Pirnmill**.

PIRNMILL

Penrioch was a farmstead of some antiquity from which the village of Pirnmill eventually grew. Apart from a history of smuggling, fishing was an important industry. The modern name of Pirnmill was derived from a mill that made bobbins, or 'pirns', from around 1780 to 1840. The ruins of the old mill can still be seen. The little village has only a few features and facilities. Listed from south to north they include: toilets, war memorial, village store and post office, The Lighthouse Café, Pirnmill Primary School and a former corrugated iron church. The beach is quite rough and bouldery.

WALK 29
Coire Fhion Lochain

Distance	9km (5.5 miles)
Height gain	650m/2130ft
Start/finish	Mid Thundergay – grid ref. 879466
Terrain	A straightforward hill walk mostly on good paths, but including a steep climb.
Refreshments	None closer than Pirnmill or Catacol.

There is a popular walk from Thundergay up to Coire Fhion Lochain, which can be extended into a short horseshoe walk on the hills overlooking the loch. Coire Fhion Lochain is sometimes rendered as Correin Lochain, which is a half-Anglicisation of the Gaelic pronunciation. While this walk is presented as a short hill walk, it can also double as an access route towards longer and tougher days on the hills. Some walkers who put in all the effort necessary to climb Meall Biorach may prefer to stay high and continue over Beinn Bhreac and Beinn Bharrain, descending to Pirnmill later, as described in Walk 28.

There is only a limited space in which to park alongside the main coastal road at **Thundergay**. The walk commences at the start of the access road serving a handful of houses at Mid Thundergay. There is a public footpath signpost reading 'Correin Lochain', a small red **postbox**, and a sign reading 'Thunderguy'. Follow the stony **access track** that winds uphill. A grassy surface continues past the last couple of houses. There are two gateways ahead and the one to pass through is the one on the right, a **kissing gate** sign-posted for 'Coire Fhion Lochain'. There is only a vague field path running uphill alongside a **fence**, but within a short while the course becomes much clearer, surfaced with stones or even crossing bare rock. Cross a ladder stile beside a gate in a tall **deer fence**.

The path runs across a heathery slope, with the dome of Meall nan Damh rising ahead. The path crosses a **burn**, then swings to the right to face Meall Biorach. An uphill pull runs alonside the **Uisge Soluis Mhóir**, which features a series of little water-falls. Chase the burn upstream following the well-constructed **path** on a parallel course. The waters of **Fion Lochan** are reached and there is a fine gravelly beach formed of broken chips of granite. Other small beaches can be distinguished by looking across the loch. Some walkers are content to come this far and retrace their steps to Thundergay, but this walk is extended around **Coire Fhion Lochain**, embracing the hills overlooking the loch.

An anti-clockwise circuit ensures that paths are easily spotted, especially paths on the steep slopes of Meall Biorach. Start the circuit by turning right along the shore of **Fion Lochan**. Follow a narrow, gritty path gently uphill and away from the shore. The path suddenly swings to the right and cuts across the steep, heathery

Lookind down on Fion Lochan and Kilbrannan Sound from the rugged crest

lower slopes of **Meall Biorach**. As it climbs, the path becomes more bouldery. Watch carefully for a turning to the left, and continue zigzagging uphill. The path takes a fairly easy course across the steep, rugged slope. At a higher level the gradient eases and there is a stretch along a level, **rounded shoulder** of low rocky outcrops, heather and gritty soil. The path crosses a large, gently sloping **slab of granite**, then rises in stages towards the main crest of the range. There is often a good view down onto Fion Lochan. A **broad summit** at 653m is covered in large boulders and short grass.

A number of vague paths converge on the bouldery summit, and by turning left the route can be continued around the head of **Coire Fhion Lochain**. There are more good views down over the loch from various points on the descent. A reasonably gentle, **rounded ridge** of outcropping slabs, gritty soil, sparse vegetation and scattered boulders is followed downhill. Later there is a steep slope of short heather leading down to a broad and boggy **gap**. Look out for a well-trodden path cutting across the gap. Turn left to follow this path down from the gap, back towards **Fion Lochan**. The path descends a rugged slope to reach the waterside, then proceeds across the foot of a heathery slope to reach the outflowing **Uisge Soluis Mhóir**. Cross over the burn and turn right to follow it downstream. The return route is simply a matter of retracing earlier steps of the day, following the path back down to **Mid Thundergay** and the access track down to the main coastal road.

THUNDERGAY

Thundergay, or Thunderguy, was one of a series of farmsteads dotted along the western side of the Isle of Arran, all of great antiquity. They included Thundergay, Penrioch, Altgobhlach, Imachar and Banleacainn. Stories relate that the tenants held their tenancy from the Scottish kings. Some are said to have obtained their tenancy from a grateful Robert the Bruce in respect of services rendered during his long and bitter campaign to secure the Scottish throne, though there is no real evidence to support this.

The little settlement of Thundergay looks across Kilbrannan Sound to Kintyre

WALK 30
Catacol and Meall nan Damh

Distance	12km (7.5 miles)
Height gain	580m/1900ft
Start/finish	Fairhaven, near Catacol – grid ref. 910489
Terrain	A steep, rugged and pathless ascent, but paths, tracks and roads are used towards the end.
Refreshments	Catacol Bay Hotel at Catacol.

Meall nan Damh raises its rugged slopes almost directly south of Catacol. An ascent of its rocky dome can be combined with a descent alongside the lovely Fion Lochan. If the ascent commences at the small car park near Fairhaven, then the descent can rejoin the main coastal road at Thundergay. If a handy bus happens to be passing, then it can be used to return to Catacol, but in any case the coastal walk along the main road is pleasant, pursuing a roller-coaster route and clinging to a rugged slope overlooking Kilbrannan Sound. It was the last part of the coastal road around the Isle of Arran to be completed, as the terrain was particularly difficult.

Fairhaven is a large white house offering accommodation a short way south of **Catacol**, where a bridge spans the river draining into Catacol Bay. There is a **car park** beside the bridge, just on the south side close to Fairhaven. Start walking immediately from the back of the car park, following a clear, grassy and stony path parallel to the river, the **Abhainn Mòr**. Go through a tall gate in a **deer fence** and cross a small campground where there is a large **wooden hut**. A narrower path continues onwards, crossing a squelchy area of heather and bog myrtle. There are a few trees on the hillside, and when the last of these have been passed, start climbing up the rugged slope.

Heather and boulders have to be negotiated without the benefit of a trodden path. The minor summit of **Meall nan Leac Sleamhuinn** can be seen at the top of the slope, and this is a useful feature to head towards at first. Later, however, the loftier dome of Meall nan Damh is seen and a course should be steered towards the ridge on its right-hand side. A rugged moorland slope and a small **burn** need to be crossed before the ridge is gained.

A steep slope of uniform heather gives way to a slightly gentler slope of **low rocky outcrops** and scattered boulders. In clear weather a fine line of jagged peaks can be seen to the left, running from Caisteal Abhail to Beinn Nuis, while far away to the right, beyond Kintyre, are the Paps of Jura. The heather underfoot gets shorter and features little clubmosses, while the gradient gradually eases. The ground becomes more bouldery as a large **cairn** is passed, although the larger summit cairn on **Meall nan Damh** is a bit further along and stands at 570m. ▶

> There are fine views all around the Isle of Arran, but your attention will be drawn to the gap beyond the moorland rise of Meall Bhig, where this route is heading.

To leave the summit of **Meall nan Damh**, pick a way downhill south-westwards and aim for a small lochan on a broad moorland gap. It is necessary to walk towards the edge of the hill before the lochan can be seen, then it is necessary to pick a careful way down the steep slope to

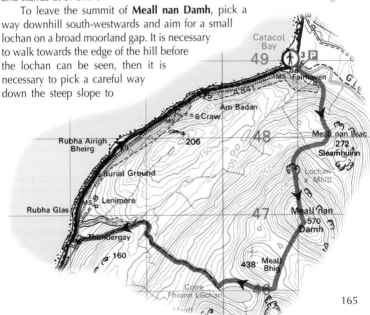

avoid extensive outcrops of rock. Pass the **lochan** on its left-hand side, just below 400m, and forge straight across a moorland slope on the eastern side of **Meall Bhig**. This tussocky bog features a narrow path leading to another small **pool** on the next gap.

There is a clear **path** cutting across the gap, so turn right to follow it into the huge hollow of **Coire Fhion Lochain**. The path descends a rugged slope to reach the waterside and there are views of three bright, gritty beaches around the shores of **Fion Lochan**. An inspection of one of these beaches, after crossing the outflow from the loch, reveals it to be made of broken chips of granite. Follow the path downstream alongside the burn called **Uisge Soluis Mhóir**. The path is well constructed as it heads downhill. Note a series of fine **waterfalls** on the descent, then watch for the path swinging to the right, crossing the **burn** as it flows downstream.

The path crosses a heathery slope and later there is a ladder stile beside a gate in a tall **deer fence**. The path crosses bare rock and stone, but at a lower level it becomes quite vague, although there is a **fence** which shows the way downhill. Go through a **kissing gate** at the bottom of the field and turn left to continue down a grassy farm access track. A couple of houses are passed in **Mid Thundergay**, while the track becomes stonier on the way down to the main coastal road.

Turn right to follow the coastal road. The first burn crossed is the **Uisge Soluis Mhóir**, which was chased downstream from Coire Fhion Lochain. The next feature of note is an old **burial ground**. The road then clings precariously to a rugged slope, sometimes having **cliffs** above or below it, featuring contorted sea stacks. There are plenty of trees clinging for survival on the upper cliffs, with heather and bracken on the lower slopes. Halfway back to Fairhaven the access track running up to **Craw** will be noticed off to the right. When **Fairhaven** is finally approached the road runs more sedately along a stretch of fairly level ground.

WALK 31
Catacol and Beinn Bhreac

Distance	17km (10.5 miles)
Height gain	1200m/3935ft
Start	Fairhaven, near Catacol – grid ref. 910489
Terrain	Rugged hill walking, often without trodden paths, so careful navigation is needed in mist.
Refreshments	Catacol Bay Hotel at Catacol.

Beinn Bhreac offers a fine, high-level walk along a smooth, whaleback ridge. The rugged dome of Meall nan Damh can be crossed as an enormous stepping stone on the way to Beann Bhreac and, after making a descent to lonely Loch Tanna, the two broad summits of Beinn Tarsuinn are included. There is a long descent into and through Glen Catacol to close the circuit. Beinn Bhreac is perched between the waters of Kilbrannan Sound and the highest peaks of Arran, so views in all directions prove most interesting in clear weather.

Fairhaven is a large white house offering accommodation a short way south of **Catacol**, where a bridge spans the river draining into Catacol Bay. There is a **car park** beside the bridge, just on the south side close to Fairhaven. Start walking immediately from the back of the car park, following a clear, grassy, stony path parallel to the river, the **Abhainn Mór**. Go through a tall gate in a **deer fence** and cross a small campground where there is a large **wooden hut**. A narrower path continues onwards, crossing a squelchy area of heather and bog myrtle. There are a few trees on the hillside, and when the last of these have been passed, start climbing up the rugged slope.

Heather and boulders have to be negotiated without the benefit of a trodden path. The minor summit of **Meall**

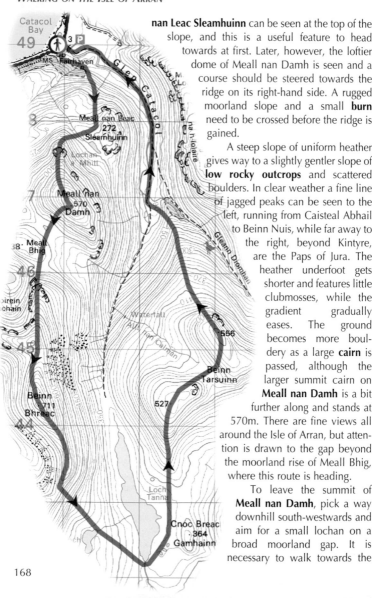

nan Leac Sleamhuinn can be seen at the top of the slope, and this is a useful feature to head towards at first. Later, however, the loftier dome of Meall nan Damh is seen and a course should be steered towards the ridge on its right-hand side. A rugged moorland slope and a small **burn** need to be crossed before the ridge is gained.

A steep slope of uniform heather gives way to a slightly gentler slope of **low rocky outcrops** and scattered boulders. In clear weather a fine line of jagged peaks can be seen to the left, running from Caisteal Abhail to Beinn Nuis, while far away to the right, beyond Kintyre, are the Paps of Jura. The heather underfoot gets shorter and features little clubmosses, while the gradient gradually eases. The ground becomes more bouldery as a large **cairn** is passed, although the larger summit cairn on **Meall nan Damh** is a bit further along and stands at 570m. There are fine views all around the Isle of Arran, but attention is drawn to the gap beyond the moorland rise of Meall Bhig, where this route is heading.

To leave the summit of **Meall nan Damh**, pick a way downhill south-westwards and aim for a small lochan on a broad moorland gap. It is necessary to walk towards the

168

Looking back along the rugged crest towards the dome of Meall nan Damh

edge of the hill before the lochan can be seen, then it is necessary to pick a careful way down the steep slope to avoid extensive **outcrops of rock**. Pass the lochan on its left-hand side, below 400m, and forge straight across a moorland slope on the eastern side of **Meall Bhig**. This tussocky bog features a narrow path leading to another small **pool** on the next gap.

There is a clear **path** cutting across the gap, but cross over it and climb straight uphill, heading southwards. A short, steep slope of short heather gives way to a gentler slope of outcropping slabs, gritty soil, sparse vegetation and boulders. Follow this **rounded shoulder** further uphill, passing to one or the other side of a wrinkled outcrop at the top. There is a **summit** at 653m where a number of vague paths converge, and there are fine views down into **Coire Fhion Lochain**. Continue straight along the rounded, bouldery crest, using a path that proves to be quite easy despite the boulders. The path leads to a large summit cairn on **Beinn Bhreac** at 711m. ▶

There is a sudden view straight ahead stretching beyond the Isle of Arran to the prominent pyramid of Ailsa Craig.

Leave the summit and continue along the rounded, bouldery ridge, following a **path** further along the ridge. The ridge levels out on a shoulder, then there are larger boulders to be crossed on the way down to the gap of **Bealach an Fharaidh**. Exit directly to the left from the gap, dropping steeply downhill on a rather steep and worn stony **path**. Anyone wanting to avoid this route could walk on the rough, bouldery slopes to either side. When the slope begins to level out, masses of prostrate juniper can be seen amid the boulders and heather. Head directly across a rugged, boggy moorland slope, passing the outflow of little **Dubh Loch** on the way to the foot of **Loch Tanna**.

Cross the **Allt Tigh an Shiorraim** where it flows from Loch Tanna, then turn left to start walking towards Beinn Tarsuinn. Following the eastern **shore** of the loch is rather too rough and wet, so it is better to drift away from the shore and head northwards towards the hills. The moorland slope can be boggy and rocky in places, and as the ground steepens there is prostrate juniper couched amid the rock and heather. The first part of Beinn Tarsuinn is broad, gritty, bouldery and features some low outcrops of granite. The only **cairn** is a small construction just off the 527m summit. Continue across the summit, down to a broad, boggy gap, then climb uphill towards a slightly higher part of **Beinn Tarsuinn**. Drift to the left on the ascent to reach the bouldery cairn on the bouldery summit at 556m. ◀

There is a fine view along a jagged line of peaks from Beinn Nuis to Caisteal Abhail, while in the opposite direction the Paps of Jura appear beyond Meall nan Damh.

Aim north-west towards Meall nan Damh at the start of the descent, dropping down a steep slope of heather and boulders. Swing more northwards towards the junction of **Glen Catacol** and **Gleann Diomhan** later, crossing a gentle, boggy slope before descending more steeply again. There is a vague path on the lower part of the descent. Swing to the left towards the end of the slope, aiming to pick up a clear **path** running through Glen Catacol.

Turn right to follow the path, which generally runs close to the river, the **Abhainn Mòr**, which in turn often runs across slabs of granite where only occasional

A view along the length of Loch Tanna towards the dome of Meall nan Damh

boulders stand marooned. Small rapids and **waterfalls** can be enjoyed. The river has a more cobbly stretch and the ground alongside features a mixture of grass, heather, bracken and bog myrtle. When the river goes through a narrow constriction, the path climbs over an outcrop of banded rock. The final meanders of the river are faithfully traced and a **ladder stile** needs to be crossed before the main road is reached at a flat concrete bridge. Turn left to cross the bridge to return to the car park near **Fairhaven** where the walk started.

CATACOL

Catacol was no more than a poor clachan in the 1800s, but the land was acquired by the Hamiltons and things began to change. The illegitimate daughter of the eighth Duke, Ann Douglas, married Lord Rossmore from Ireland and received the lands around Catacol as a dowry. Lord Rossmore built a fine house where Catacol Farm now stands, as well as a church at Lenimore. There was no minister for the church at first, but when one was appointed a manse was built where the Catacol Hotel now stands. The terrace of cottages known as the Twelve Apostles was built in the 1860s to house the people who were cleared from the older clachan. However, the people refused to live there and drifted elsewhere, and the terrace became known as Hungry Row until tenants were found. Facilities in the village are limited to the food, drink and accommodation provided by the Catacol Bay Hotel.

WALK 32
Catacol and Beinn Tarsuinn

Distance	17km (10.5 miles)
Height gain	910m/2985ft
Start	Fairhaven, near Catacol – grid ref. 910489
Terrain	Rugged hill walking, often without trodden paths.
Refreshments	Catacol Bay Hotel at Catacol.

Glen Catacol offers splendid access to the hills in the north-west of the Isle of Arran. While many walkers feel obliged to climb the highest hills, there are a handful of lesser heights that prove to be just as rugged, if not more so in places. The sprawling Beinn Tarsuinn can be climbed, followed by the steep and bouldery slopes of Beinn Bhreac. The broad moorland crest beyond is punctuated by the little hump of Beinn Bhiorach and the larger hump of Meall Mòr. At the end of the walk, there is a splendid view along the length of Glen Catacol, not available from any other standpoint. The lack of paths across these hills suggests that most walkers are content to stay low in the glens, or on the higher mountains.

Fairhaven is a large white house a short way south of the village of **Catacol**, where a bridge spans the river draining Glen Catacol. There is a **car park** beside the bridge, just on the south side near Fairhaven. Start walking by crossing the bridge and turning right. A public footpath signpost offers destinations including Gleann Diomhan and Loch Tanna. Follow a broad, grassy, stony path alongside the river, the **Abhainn Mór**, and cross a ladder stile over a tall **deer fence**. The path continues to run alongside the river, then rises to cross an outcrop of banded rock. The river runs through a narrow constriction below the outcrop. The path runs alongside a cobbly stretch of the river, passing areas of grass, heather, bracken and bog myrtle.

Further upstream, the river runs in rapids and **waterfalls** across bare slabs of granite where occasional large boulders stand marooned. There are a couple of lesser paths branching off to the left leading up into **Gleann Diomhan**, but don't follow them. A bouldery river needs to be forded and the path remains clear as it climbs towards the head of **Glen Catacol**. The surface is rather more bouldery and some sections can be boggy. The river often features small waterfalls and there are lengthy stretches where the water slides over a clean bed of granite. Off to the left is a steeper waterslide on the **Allt nan Calman**. Follow the river upstream as it diminishes, passing a sprawling cairn before reaching another cairn

173

There is a fine view along a jagged line of peaks from Beinn Nuis to Caisteal Abhail, while in the opposite direction the Paps of Jura appear beyond Meal nan Damh.

on a broad, stony **gap** over 330m. There is a view ahead of **Loch Tanna**, the largest and most remote lake on Arran.

Turn left to climb above the **gap** (ascending a steep slope of heather and boulders) before the gradient eases and there are fewer boulders. At length a small **cairn** is passed on an outcrop of granite slabs, though this is not quite on the 527m summit of Beinn Tarsuinn. The rest of the summit area is a broad expanse of low outcrops, boulders and gritty soil. Continue walking northeastwards across the summit, drop down to a broad gap, then climb uphill towards a slightly higher summit on **Beinn Tarsuinn**. Drift to the left on the ascent to reach the cairn on the bouldery summit at 556m. ◀

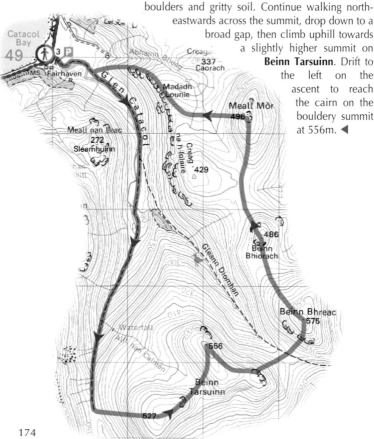

174

The next summit is Beinn Bhreac, but it should not be approached directly across Gleann Diomhan. Instead, walk south-eastwards along the crest of **Beinn Tarsuinn**, then gradually drift to the left until the direction is almost north-eastwards. There is a steep and bouldery descent from the crest of Beinn Tarsuinn to a broad **gap** of boggy ground and stony patches over 400m.

Immediately ahead is the steep, intimidating, bouldery flank of Beinn Bhreac. The heather is quite deep and springy, interspersed with bilberry and crowberry, often concealing **deep holes** that need to be avoided. The **bouldery** parts of the slope need great care as some of the specimens are loose. On many parts it is necessary to use hands as well as feet to assist on the climb. The gradient eases near the top, with shorter heather, short grass and more deeply embedded boulders. The bouldery summit cairn on **Beinn Bhreac** stands at 575m.

Leave the top of Beinn Bhreac by walking north-west along a broad, rounded ridge, before swinging more northwards toward the rugged hump of Beinn Bhiorach. On the descent from Beinn Bhreac, a large, square **cairn** is passed, then after crossing a broad moorland **gap** a short climb leads up an easy, bouldery slope. The top of **Beinn Bhiorach** is a bare peak of rock at 486m. Continue walking over to the next **broad gap**, carefully picking a way down a short, steep slope which has some rocky

Meall nan Damh is seen from a broad and boggy gap below Beinn Tarsuinn

areas. The next prominent hill in view is Meall Mòr, and this is best approached by taking a direct line across an uneven slope of moorland. Climb straight up a blunt, **rounded ridge**, where scattered boulders on the heathery slope pose no problem. There is a cairn on the summit of **Meall Mòr** at 496m, with another cairn further along the crest. There is a last chance to absorb the view before the descent.

Descend westwards from the summit, picking a careful way down a steep slope of heather, avoiding any areas of rock. Forge across an uneven tract of moorland, crossing a shallow valley and drifting to the right to reach the prow of **Madadh Lounie**. The rugged moorland underfoot gives way to a rounded spur of short heather descending more steeply into **Glen Catacol**. ◀ Descend more steeply, bearing to the right along a **narrow path** to avoid a rock-step to the left. The path descends through a **notch** in the rock, then continues down a slope of bracken, later passing close to a **large boulder** of granite. The gradient eases and by heading towards the river you can join the path that was used at the start of the day's walk. Follow the path alongside the river, crossing the **ladder stile** over the tall deer fence, to return to the main road and car park across the bridge near **Fairhaven**.

There is a splendid view along the length of the glen, which in its middle reaches is a perfect 'U' shape.

WALK 33
Lochranza and Meall Mòr

Distance	11km (6.5 miles)
Height gain	500m/1640ft
Start	Lochranza Castle – grid ref. 932507
Terrain	Roads at first, then paths, giving way to rugged, pathless terrain.
Refreshments	Lochranza Hotel and a sandwich bar in Lochranza, Catacol Bay Hotel at Catacol, restaurant at the Arran Distillery.

Rising south of Lochranza is a rugged, rocky dome of a hill called Meall Mòr. While a direct approach would be quite difficult, the hill can be climbed more easily on the way from Glen Catacol to Gleann Easan Biorach. The main coastal road is followed from Lochranza to Catacol, although of course this could be covered using bus services if desired. Fine views are available on the ascent, though much of the upland moorland is quite rough and pathless, needing special care in mist. The descent and return to Lochranza is by way of the boggy Gleann Easan Biorach.

The start of this walk could be anywhere in **Lochranza**, but Lochranza Castle makes a good reference point. Walk through the village in the direction of the **Claonaig Ferry** and continue along the main coastal road to leave the village.

WAR GRAVE

A monument near the Claonaig Ferry slipway has been erected to comemmorate the crew of a submarine which sank offshore during World War II. The inscription reads: 'HMS/M Vandal sank 1½ miles north west from here on 24th February 1943. She and her crew lie there still.'

The road runs round **Coillemore Point** and there is a track running parallel to the road just a short way inland. Follow the track, which passes a moss-bound heap of stones marked with the following words: 'The Sailor's Grave. Here Lies John McLean. Died 12 August 1854.' Follow the road past a **solitary house**. A rugged, vegetated, damp and wooded cliff rises above the road. There are a few small, damp caves and the cliff is a favourite nesting place for seabirds.

Passing through **Catacol**, note the Catacol Bay Hotel and the terrace of cottages known as the **Twelve Apostles**. Leaving the village, there is a choice either of walking along the main road, or walking along the grassy and pebbly strip between the main road and the sea. Either way, a flat concrete bridge will be reached close to the large white house called **Fairhaven**. Don't cross the bridge, but turn left to leave the road and follow a path into **Glen Catacol**, as indicated by a public footpath signpost. Follow a broad, grassy and stony path alongside the river and cross a **ladder stile** over a tall deer fence. The path continues to run alongside the river, the **Abhainn Mòr**, then rises to cross an outcrop of banded rock. The river runs through a narrow constriction below the outcrop. The path runs alongside a cobbly stretch of the river, passing areas of grass, heather, bracken and bog myrtle.

When the open floor of the glen is reached, drift leftwards away from the riverside path. Aim to walk through an area of bracken in the direction of the rocky prow of Madadh Lounie, passing a prominent **large boulder** on the way. A **narrow path** should be located, which leaves the brackeny slope and climbs up through a **notch** in the rock above. Keep strictly to the line of the path to negotiate the ascent of a **rock-step**. Once on top, note the splendid view along the length of Glen Catacol, which in its middle reaches is a perfect 'U' shape. Continue climbing up a rounded spur of short heather, which gives way to more rugged moorland at a

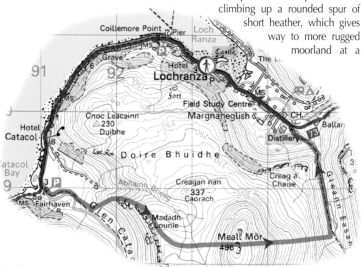

The Twelve Apostles are a row of estate cottages beside the road at Catacol

higher level. Leaving **Madadh Lounie**, it is necessary to forge straight across an uneven tract of moorland in the direction of Meall Mòr. Looking ahead, pick any line of ascent towards the summit which seems to be free of rock. There are some strips of heather which allow steep, but relatively safe ascents. There is a cairn on the summit of **Meall Mòr** at 496m, with another cairn further along the crest. Take a moment to savour the view before the descent, which is remarkably extensive despite the modest elevation.

Walk roughly eastwards to descend from **Meall Mòr**. The slope has outcrops of rock and boulders at first, though these begin to give way to more rugged, boggy moorland slopes. There are no paths on the way into **Gleann Easan Biorach**, and it is necessary to keep looking ahead to gauge the best line of descent. It is perhaps best to drift slightly to the left, in order to avoid being drawn into a **watercourse** which is mostly bare rock, but keep looking ahead in order to outflank any obstacles in good time. Eventually, a **path** will be reached which runs roughly parallel to the river draining the glen. Turn left to follow it downstream.

Enjoy a series of little **waterfalls** on the way down through **Gleann Easan Biorach**. The path often crosses boggy ground and squelchy grassland, but inflowing burns offer the chance to get your boots cleaned from time to time. A firmer path is eventually joined where the river drops more steeply through a **rocky gorge**. Small waterfalls and rock pools are overlooked by the rocky dome of **Torr Nead an Eoin**. A stretch of safety fencing has been provided above a small water intake. The rocky path gives way to a **broad track**, which runs between a bridge and a cottage to reach the main road near the **Isle of Arran Distillery**.

ISLE OF ARRAN DISTILLERY

Completed only in 1997, the Isle of Arran Distillery buildings are quite modern, yet have distinctly traditional roofing. When the enterprise was being promoted, it was claimed to be the first legal distillery on the island for 160 years. Some claim that when whisky was last distilled on the Isle of Arran it was the best in Scotland. Connoisseurs can now judge for themselves, testing the single malts against others in Scotland. The distillery caters for visitors by offering tours, and incorporates a gift shop and restaurant. For details ☎ 01770 830264 or see the website www.arranwhisky.com.

Turn left to walk back through **Lochranza**, passing first the Isle of Arran Distillery, then later the campsite, Loch Ranza Field Studies Centre, St. Bride's Church and **youth hostel** to return to **Lochranza Castle**, or wherever else you may have commenced the walk.

LOCHRANZA CASTLE

There are two parts to Lochranza Castle. First there was a medieval hall-house, with a heavily defended lower doorway and an upper doorway with a removable ladder. The owner may have been Sween, who married into the royal house of Connacht and was Lord of Knapdale in Argyll. When Robert the High Steward became King of Scotland in 1371, Lochranza became a royal castle. A later period of building incorporated Sween's castle into a rather more decorative structure. The building was completed by one of the Montgomery Earls of Eglinton, who had received estates on the Isle of Arran from James II in 1452. New doorways were created and old ones were blocked, and this remains apparent from a close study of the fabric. The Montgomerys lost their estates to the Hamiltons in 1705 and much later the castle fell to ruins. One whole corner collapsed during a storm in 1897, but the fabric has now been consolidated and has plenty of interesting features and poky corners to explore.

WALK 34
Gleann Easan Biorach

Distance	16km (10 miles)
Height gain	410m/1345ft
Start/finish	Lochranza Castle – grid ref. 932507
Terrain	Mostly rough, boggy, bouldery paths often running alongside rivers and burns.
Refreshments	Restaurant at the Arran Distillery, Catacol Bay Hotel at Catacol, a sandwich bar and Lochranza Hotel in Lochranza.

There is a popular circuit into the hills of northern Arran from Lochranza to Catacol. The route doesn't climb any hills, but works its way through the glens and over a couple of bleak and boggy gaps. Starting from Lochranza, the route climbs up through Gleann Easan Biorach to reach Loch na Davie, then climbs over a gap on the slopes of Beinn Bhreac before descending through Gleann Diomhan and Glen Catacol. The main coastal road can be used to make a circular walk, leading from the village of Catacol back to Lochranza. The paths in Gleann Easan Biorach, Glen Catacol and Gleann Diomhan can be used to reach a variety of hills in the north-west of the Isle of Arran. Some of these hills are covered in other route descriptions in this guide. This walk covers only the basic circuit from glen to glen.

The start of this walk could be anywhere in **Lochranza**, but Lochranza Castle makes a good reference point. Walk through the long and straggly village as if following the road over to Sannox, passing the **youth hostel**, St. Bride's Church, Loch Ranza Field Studies Centre and the **Isle of Arran Distillery**.

Just beyond the distillery, and immediately before a humpback bridge, is a public footpath signpost on the right. The signpost points the way into **Gleann Easan Biorach** and a smaller sign announces that this is also the

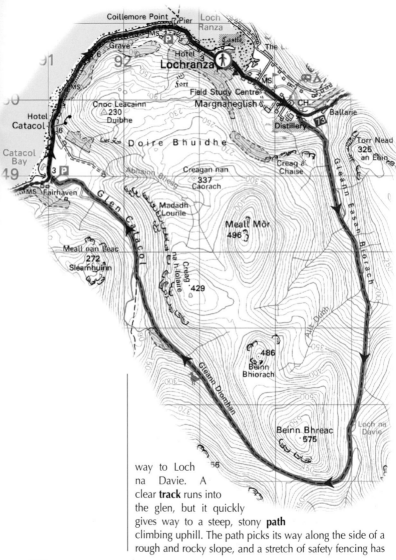

way to Loch
na Davie. A
clear **track** runs into
the glen, but it quickly
gives way to a steep, stony **path**
climbing uphill. The path picks its way along the side of a
rough and rocky slope, and a stretch of safety fencing has

After leaving the Isle of Arran Distillery a path leads into Gleann Easan Biorach

been provided above a small water intake point. A series of small **waterfalls** and rock pools are overlooked by the rocky dome of **Torr Nead an Eoin**. The path continues climbing and eventually runs more or less level across a broad and boggy moorland close to the river.

There are other small waterfalls to look at as the path runs further alongside the river. The path often crosses **boggy ground** and squelchy grassland, but inflowing burns offer the chance to get your boots cleaned from time to time. The river often slides along a smooth bed of granite, and there is a tributary off to the left that has the same sort of appearance. The path then climbs uphill on a bouldery, heathery slope, and in wet weather it may well carry running water. The climb leads up to a heathery gap over 360m where the shallow waters of **Loch na Davie** can be seen to the left. Dozens of small boulders project from the water, while careful inspection of either end of the loch reveals that the water dribbles in opposite directions both into Gleann Easan Biorach and Glen Iorsa.

The path continues beyond **Loch na Davie**, passing a cairn and gradually swinging to the right to climb up around the shoulders of **Beinn Bhreac**. A couple of smaller cairns help to keep walkers on course at times when the path becomes rather narrow and vague. There is a gradual climb to reach a broad, boggy and stony **gap** over 400m between Beinn Bhreac, to the right, and Beinn Tarsuinn, to the left. In mist, it is helpful to spot the start of the path leading down into the top end of **Gleann Diomhan**, just to be sure that the correct line is going to be followed later. There is a narrow, stony path running parallel to the burn on the eastern side. Anyone inadvertently walking along the western side will experience great difficulties later. On the way downhill, the path is quite rugged in places. A stepped series of small **waterfalls** are followed by a longer fall tucked out of sight of the path. A granite gorge leads through an area that has been surrounded by a tall deer fence. This is the **Gleann Diomhan National Nature Reserve**, and the fence has been erected to keep deer and sheep from damaging or destroying rare tree species.

GLEANN DIOMHAN NATIONAL NATURE RESERVE

The securely fenced enclosure high in Gleann Diomhan seems incongruous in its wilderness setting, but it is necessary to prevent sheep and deer from damaging two rare species of tree which thrive there. Sorbus arranensis and Sorbus pseudo-fennicus both have a roothold in the glen. They are whitebeam, or service trees, of the same genus as the rowan, bearing clusters of berries when in fruit. They grow apparently from bare rock, needing very little soil to secure a root-hold. These two species are unique to the Isle of Arran and are therefore given the protection of a secure fence against grazing animals. A ladder stile allows access to walkers who wish to explore further.

Continue along the rough path beside the **deer fence**. The path leaves the lower corner of the enclosure and begins to swing to the right as it leaves the glen. The ground becomes firmer and drier, especially when areas of bracken are crossed. The path descends into **Glen Catacol** and joins a firm, clear path, which is followed by turning right. The path generally runs close to the river, the **Abhainn Mòr**, which itself often runs across slabs of granite where only occasional boulders stand marooned. Small rapids and **waterfalls** can be enjoyed. The river has a more cobbly stretch and the ground alongside features a mixture of grass, heather, bracken and bog myrtle.

The river goes through a narrow constriction, while the path climbs over an outcrop of banded rock. The final meanders of the river are faithfully traced and a **ladder stile** needs to be crossed before the main road is reached at a flat concrete **bridge**. There is a public footpath signpost pointing back into the glen, a car park just across the bridge, and a pebbly raised beach across the road hidden behind gorse bushes. Turn right to follow the main road towards the village of **Catacol**, or alternatively walk on the grass or pebbles along the shore. Pass the cottages known as the **Twelve Apostles**, as well as the **Catacol Bay Hotel**. ▶

Some walkers might like to arrange to be collected at Catacol, or wait for a bus to Lochranza, but others will enjoy the short and easy walk between the two villages.

Houses look across the road to a rocky shore, while later the shore is more bouldery. Inland, a rugged, vegetated, damp and wooded cliff rises above the road. There are a few small, damp caves and the cliff is a favourite nesting place for seabirds. Pass a **solitary house**, then later take a short **grassy track** to the right of the road, staying at the foot of the wooded cliff. A moss-bound heap of stones is marked with the following words: 'The Sailor's Grave. Here Lies John McLean. Died 12 August 1854.' Continue following the road round **Coillemore Point**, passing toilets, car parking spaces and the **Claonaig Ferry**. The road continues through the village of **Lochranza**, returning walkers to **Lochranza Castle**, or wherever the walk was started.

LOCHRANZA

The long and straggly village of Lochranza sits beside a sea loch and for a long time the only real access was from the sea. It was named Ranza by Norse settlers, while Scott penned poetry about it in Lord of the Isles. There is a fine range of features and facilities. Working southwards through the village from the Claonaig Ferry slipway these include: toilets, sandwich bar, butcher, a couple of bed and breakfasts, Lochranza Hotel and Boguillie Bar. Next comes Lochranza Castle, a couple more bed and breakfasts, Lochranza and Catacol Village Hall and Lochranza Youth Hostel. These are followed by St. Bride's Church, a surgery, Loch Ranza Field Studies Centre, Apple Lodge Guest House, Lochranza Golf Club, caravan and camp site with shop, fire station and finally the Arran Distillery, with its gift shop and restaurant. Walkers who complete the full circuit described above will pass everything.

WALK 35
Lochranza and the Cock of Arran

Distance	13km (8 miles)
Height gain	360m/1180ft
Start/finish	St. Bride's Church, Lochranza – grid ref. 937503
Terrain	Roads, tracks and rugged coastal paths. Some parts can be muddy and rocky.
Refreshments	Lochranza Hotel and a sandwich bar in Lochranza, restaurant at the Isle of Arran Distillery.

The walk around the Cock of Arran from Lochranza is one of the classic coastal walks on the Isle of Arran. Lochranza is a long and straggly village that sits beside a charming sea loch. The romantic Lochranza Castle overlooks the waters from a narrow, grassy, pebbly point. The walk around the coast could be structured to link Lochranza with the distant village of Sannox, but this particular route description heads only for the remote Laggan Cottage, then crosses back over the hills to return to Lochranza. The rest of the coastal walk is covered on Walk 37, in a circuit based on Sannox.

The walk could be started anywhere in the straggly village of **Lochranza**, but for the purpose of defining a place, start near **St. Bride's Church** or the Loch Ranza Field Studies Centre. There is a signpost beside the road at this point indicating such varied destinations as the Fairy Dell, Ossian's Cave, the Cock of Arran and Laggan. Follow the minor road past the **Lochranza Surgery**, crossing a bridge and continuing past a **golf course**. At a junction with another minor road there are two public footpath signposts. Turn left to follow the road past some cottages to reach a pebbly beach at the head of **Loch Ranza**. Almost immediately on reaching the beach, turn right along a stony track. This quickly turns left and proceeds uphill between lines of

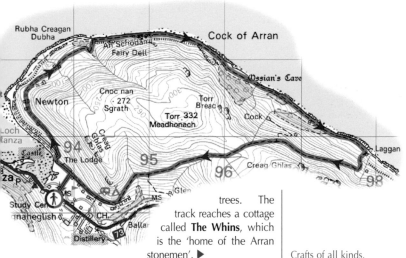

trees. The track reaches a cottage called **The Whins**, which is the 'home of the Arran stonemen'. ▶

The track continues across a rugged slope of bracken and gorse scrub. Keep left to follow a track downhill towards a cottage called **The Knowe**. Ford a small burn below the cottage and continue along a moorland path. This runs down to a cottage and wooden hut beside the sea at the foot of the wooded **Fairy Dell**. Turn right to walk along a coastal path, where short green grass offers an easy surface between bracken and the rugged shore. Later, a **huge boulder** is passed and there is little difference between walking on the beach or on the slope above it; both are littered with large boulders of coarse conglomerate rock. This area is known as the **Scriodan**. Either follow the most well-trodden line between the boulders, or if the tide is out, then there might be an easier way along the beach.

After wrestling with the boulders, there is an easier stretch of path and another **large boulder** features an overhanging projection, which is good enough to offer protection from the rain. The coastal path continues easily along another ribbon of short green grass, and the ruins of a couple of **stone huts** might be noticed in the

Crafts of all kinds, but especially decorated stones, are available for purchase.

A view over the sea inlet of Loch Ranza on the way round to the Cock of Arran

bracken alongside. There is one level stretch that has been used as a field in the past, and curiously there is a natural **igneous dyke** forming a boundary wall between the field and the beach. The path crosses a drystone wall belonging to **Cock Farm**, whose ruins are out of sight further uphill. Also out of sight uphill is **Ossian's Cave**. Keep to the path closest to the rocky shore, taking care over ankle-wrenching and muddy terrain.

Some **ruined buildings** beside the sea once housed a little industrial site where coal was mined and saltpans were in use. The path crosses another rocky area, but gets a little easier later. Look out for a roughed-out circular **millstone** complete with a central hole just to the left of the path. The white form of **Laggan Cottage** appears quite suddenly after crossing a low outcrop of rock. Leave the isolated cottage by walking straight uphill, passing alongside its former kitchen garden.

The path is a clear, grassy ribbon that zigzags uphill between areas of bracken. There are some drystone-walled **enclosures** off to the left, then the path swings to the right and cuts across a steep and roughly vegetated slope. Looking downhill the ruins of **Cock Farm** and its old fields can be seen.

As the path climbs it is flanked by heather and its surface becomes quite stony. At the top of the path there is a broad moorland **gap** to be crossed, where a **cairn**

COCK FARM

The tumbled remains of Cock Farm are a sad reminder of how well populated the Isle of Arran once was. There were once over a hundred people living in the area now enclosed by Laggan and Cock Farm, yet not a single person lives there now. Cock Farm's greatest claim to fame concerns the Macmillan family. Malcolm Macmillan was born there in 1735 and he was the grandfather of Daniel Macmillan who founded the famous Macmillan publishing house. Malcolm was therefore the great-great grandfather of the Prime Minister Harold Macmillan. Cock Farm was finally deserted in 1912 and now lies mouldering in a brackeny hollow.

stands beside the path at 263m. The path is flanked by boggy ground on its downhill run, surfaced with stones in some parts and crossing bare rock in other parts. There is generally a view over the **Isle of Arran Distillery** all the way downhill. The only time this passes from view is where the path nips into a wooded ravine to cross a small burn using a **footbridge**. The path runs down onto a clear, broad **track** and turns right. The track continues gently downhill, eventually passing the entrance to **Butt Lodge**, which was once used by shooting parties and later served as a hotel. Turn left along the **minor road** used at the start of the walk, crossing the **golf course** and bridge to return to the main road near **St. Bride's Church** and the field studies centre.

A path leads down to Lochranza with Torr Nead an Eion and Meall Mór in view

WALK 36
Lochranza and Sail an Im

Distance	17km (10.5 miles)
Height gain	920m/3020ft
Start/finish	Isle of Arran Distillery, Lochranza – grid ref. 493497
Terrain	Good paths at first, then pathless moorland slopes.
Refreshments	Restaurant at the Isle of Arran Distillery.

Few walkers would consider climbing Sail an Im without continuing along the fine mountain ridge to the summit of Caisteal Abhail. Even fewer walkers would consider climbing Sail an Im from Lochranza. In fact, there is an entertaining circuit available, which uses traces of an old road over the Boguillie, linking Glen Chalmadale with North Glen Sannox. Sail an Im can then be climbed from the glen, with a return to Lochranza made directly along the broad moorland crest terminating at Torr Nead an Eoin. There is a surprise view of the village and the sea loch before the final descent.

Start at the **Isle of Arran Distillery**, set well back from the sea at **Lochranza**. Follow the main road uphill from a humpback bridge, passing the farm of **Ballarie** while skirting round the lower slopes of Torr Nead an Eoin. Turn left and follow a **farm access track** downhill, either fording the river in **Glen Chalmadale**, or crossing an adjacent footbridge. Turn right to follow the river upstream, walking along a track, passing a **building** and continuing along a path. The aim is to pick up the course of an old road running up through the glen, but its course is unclear at first. Follow the river upstream, until forced uphill to pass a pronounced bend where there is a short, steep, wooded slope. A clearer **path** continues immediately beyond.

The old highway shows some traces of engineering, but is little trodden these days and some parts are quite vague. The old way rises roughly parallel to the current main road, but on the opposite side of the river. The path rises gently across a slope of grass, bracken and heather. A handful of **stunted trees** are passed, then three small **burns** are crossed as the path continues to rise. A fourth burn is more powerful and could result in wet feet after wet weather. The burn is filled with trees and fine **waterfalls**. The path continues a little more steeply uphill, now climbing above the level of the main road over the **Boguillie**, but the gradient quickly eases on the higher moorlands and it crosses another path. The way ahead can be vague in places, crossing areas of grass and heather, but with care it is possible to distinguish the route.

The path is little more than a **groove** contouring across the moorland around 250m. It climbs a little to cross a runnel of water, then drops downhill to pass the lower corner of a **fenced enclosure**. The groove is little more than a boggy trough in places, but it is sometimes flanked by boulders and can be quite clear. A couple of little burns are crossed by their original **stone slab bridges**, and an outcrop of bedrock has a splash of white quartz. The old track turns downhill as a clear ribbon of boggy grass across a rugged moorland slope. The track may carry running water for a while, then there is a **paved ford** through a small burn. The route contours for a while across a steeper slope, then a right turn leads downhill, twisting and turning, but in the main heading straight towards **North Glen Sannox**. Aim for the river at the point where it is crossed a road bridge.

There is a **car park** across the bridge, and a riverside path leaves it to run alongside **North Sannox Burn**. Note the fine waterfall pouring beneath the bridge, before following a good path flanked by grass, heather and bog myrtle. A couple of small burns need to be forded, then there is a **tall gate** in a deer fence. The path is wet and muddy as it runs between a stand of forest and the river, passing many fine **waterfalls** as it climbs. There is a **ladder stile** leaving the top edge of the forest and the path continues upstream, with fine views of Caisteal Abhail

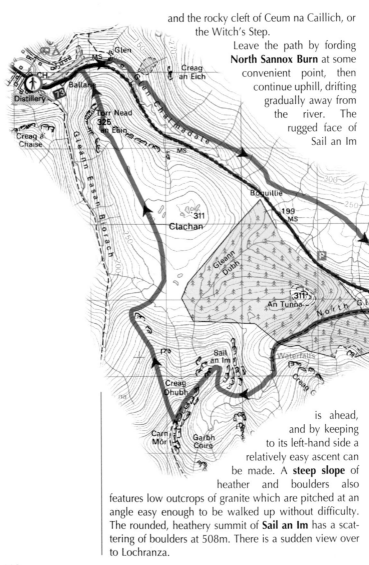

and the rocky cleft of Ceum na Caillich, or the Witch's Step.

Leave the path by fording **North Sannox Burn** at some convenient point, then continue uphill, drifting gradually away from the river. The rugged face of Sail an Im

is ahead, and by keeping to its left-hand side a relatively easy ascent can be made. A **steep slope** of heather and boulders also features low outcrops of granite which are pitched at an angle easy enough to be walked up without difficulty. The rounded, heathery summit of **Sail an Im** has a scattering of boulders at 508m. There is a sudden view over to Lochranza.

Turn left to pick up a **narrow path** which runs roughly south-west along the rounded ridge. The climb is on grass and heather, with some boulders and ribs of granite. Climb until a rounded granite hump is reached on top of the buttress of **Creag Dubh**, overlooking the Garbh Choire at 644m. While it is possible to continue along the ridge to the summit of **Caisteal Abhail**, this route now changes course and proceeds directly back to Lochranza.

Head downhill, roughly north-north-west as if dropping into Gleann Easan Biorach. In clear weather it is worth surveying the terrain from a good height before negotiating it. Start the descent by dropping down a slope of grass, heather and boulders. The terrain is actually fairly easy at first, but later there is a swing to the right and a steeper fall towards a broad, **boggy gap** high above the glen. A number of paths can be seen cutting across the bleak moorland slope, and any of them might be used. Crossing the broad gap is usually wet underfoot and there are a handful of small burns to be forded. There is a slight ascent on an uneven heathery moorland, touching 300m at **Clachan**. There are small pools to be avoided and in clear weather the hump of Torr Nead an Eoin can be seen at the end of the broad crest.

When **Torr Nead an Eoin** is finally climbed, a short ascent reveals a couple of **small cairns**, at 325m, overlooking Lochranza. It is worth walking a little further in the direction of Lochranza to enjoy a splendid bird's-eye view of the village, but note that it is not possible to make a direct descent as there are steep slopes of rock and little cliffs tucked out of sight. More distant views encompass much of northern Arran, as well as looking across to the Paps of Jura beyond Kintyre.

The final descent should be made in the direction of a solitary white **farmhouse** seen across the main road well to the right. The steep slope features short vegetation, although there is bracken at a lower level. A narrow

There is a fine aerial view of Lochranza from the summit of Torr Nead an Eoin

See Walk 33 for information about the distillery

path can be joined running alongside a **fence**. Keep to the right-hand side of it to walk straight down to the main road. Turn left down the road, reaching the **Isle of Arran Distillery** on the way back towards **Lochranza**. ◀

THE BOGUILLIE

The 'new' road over the Boguillie was constructed between Lochranza and Sannox in 1843. Up to that point most traffic reaching Lochranza came from the sea; the tracks eastwards over the Boguillie or southwards via the Craw were simply too rough and narrow to travel easily. Even when the 'new' road was built, there were fords rather than bridges, and it was barely possible for two carts to pass each other.

WALK 37
Sannox and Fionn Bhealach

Distance	16km (10 miles)
Height gain	500m/1640ft
Start/finish	North Sannox picnic area – grid ref. 015466
Terrain	Coastal tracks and paths, followed by moorlands with some clear paths and tracks.
Refreshments	Corrie Golf Club tearoom and Sannox Bay Hotel off-route at Sannox.

The coastal walk around the northern part of Arran is a popular excursion. It is possible to walk all the way from Sannox to Lochranza along rugged coastal paths, but the route described below is a circular tour, taking in the Fallen Rocks, Millstone Point and Laggan Cottage, coming back over the top of Fionn Bhealach. The course of an old highway can be traced back towards Sannox, running parallel to the main road over the Boguillie. The picnic area at the start of the walk is near Lag nan Sasunnach, where Cromwellian soldiers, killed in battle at Clach a' Chath, are said to be buried. This walk could be extended either along the coast to Lochranza, or after climbing up from Laggan Cottage, a descent could be made along a clear path and track to Lochranza with reference to Walk 35.

Start at the **North Sannox Picnic Area**, signposted off the main road just above Sannox on the way to Lochranza. There is a **car park** at the end of a short minor road, beside the sea. Anyone arriving by bus can easily walk the distance to the sea from the main road. There are picnic tables and toilets available. A **track** continues from the end of the tarmac road and enters a forest using a **tall gate** in a deer fence. Follow the track along what is actually a raised beach covered in vegetation. A mixture of deciduous trees screen views of the more regimented forest beyond. A rugged **rock-face** in the trees was once the coastline and has some small caves and undercut parts. Pass a prominent **marker pole**, which actually indicates a 'measured mile' used for speed trials at sea, and follow an electricity transmission line to the edge of the forest.

Cross a **ladder stile** beside a gate in a tall deer fence then follow the path onwards to cross an outcrop of conglomerate rock. The path continues easily through the **Fallen Rocks** – a chaotic jumble of massive conglomerate boulders strewn between a high cliff and the sea. Follow the path beyond the boulders, still tracing the electricity transmission line onwards. The poles eventually run uphill towards another **marker post**, high in

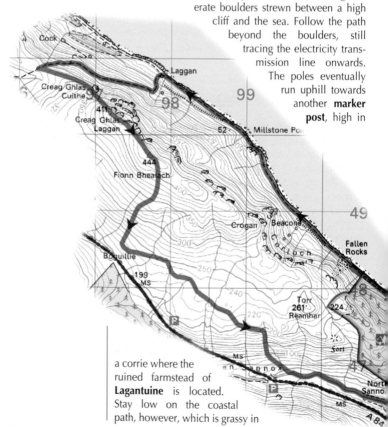

a corrie where the ruined farmstead of **Lagantuine** is located. Stay low on the coastal path, however, which is grassy in most places, but pebbly, wet or muddy in other places. There are a series of **small caves** just above the path. The first cave is quite roomy and shows obvious signs of having been used for overnight accommodation. The others are smaller and unsuitable for human occupancy. **Millstone Point** is eventually turned and the little white-washed **Laggan Cottage** will be seen ahead. The path remains easy all the way to the cottage.

Turn left uphill from what was once the kitchen garden at the cottage. The path is a clear, grassy ribbon that zigzags uphill between areas of bracken. There are some drystone-walled **enclosures** off to the left, then the path swings to the right and cuts across a steep and roughly vegetated slope. Looking downhill the ruins of **Cock Farm** and its old fields can be seen.

COCK FARM

The tumbled remains of Cock Farm are a sad reminder of how well populated the Isle of Arran once was. There were once over a hundred people living in the area now enclosed by Laggan and Cock Farm, yet not a single person lives there now. Cock Farm's greatest claim to fame concerns the Macmillan family. Malcolm Macmillan was born there in 1735 and he was the grandfather of Daniel Macmillan who founded the famous Macmillan publishing house. Malcolm was therefore the great-great grandfather of the Prime Minister Harold Macmillan. Cock Farm was finally deserted in 1912 and now lies mouldering in a brackeny hollow.

As the path climbs it is flanked by heather and its surface becomes quite stony. At the top of the path there is a broad moorland **gap** to be crossed, where a **cairn** stands beside the path at 263m. The path is flanked by boggy ground, and you turn left to leave it, walking along a heather and grass **moorland crest**. By walking close to the edge overlooking the sea, it is possible to use vague sheep paths, or quad bike tracks, but it is just as easy to stay on the crest and aim more directly for the top of **Fionn**

A path runs down-stream beside North Sannox Burn to return to North Sannox

Bhealach. There is a rounded rise at 411m before the main summit is reached, bearing a trig point at 444m. Continue along the moorland crest to start the descent, but head off to the right before reaching a **gap** followed by another broad rise. Pick a way down the rugged moorland slope, crossing areas of heather and grass which may be boggy in places. A **path** marked on some maps has been broadened by quad bike use, and it is quite clearly defined as it heads down towards the road at the **Boguillie**.

While it is indeed possible to walk straight down to the road at the Boguillie and head straight back towards Sannox, there is also another route that could be sampled. There are traces of a former highway running parallel to the main road, but at a higher level on the hillside. The course of the **old track** is not too clear on the descent from Fionn Bhealach, but if a **groove** is spotted to the left, near a boulder, then this is the line to follow.

The groove contours across the moorland around 250m. It climbs a little to cross a runnel of water, then drops downhill to pass the lower corner of a **fenced enclosure**. The groove is little more than a boggy trough in places, but it is sometimes flanked by boulders and can be quite clear. A couple of little burns are crossed by their original **stone slab bridges**, and an outcrop of bedrock has a splash of white quartz. The old track turns downhill as a clear ribbon of boggy grass across a rugged moorland slope. The track may carry running water for a while, then there is a **paved ford** through a small burn. The route contours for a while across a steeper slope, then a right turn leads downhill, twisting and turning, but in the main heading straight towards **North Glen Sannox**. Aim for the river well to the left of the point where it is crossed a road bridge, to reach the bottom corner of a **deer fence**.

Turn left to follow a **riverside path**, alongside the tall deer fence, eventually passing below the farm at **North Sannox**. Pony trekking is offered and there are always a variety of horses, ponies and even donkeys grazing in the fields. Follow the farm access road to a minor road at a **bridge**. Either turn left to return to the **North Sannox picnic area** and car park, or turn right to reach the main road and its bus services. The nearest places offering food and drink are in the village of Sannox.

SANNOX

The Sannox area is one of many places on the Isle of Arran with abundant ancient remains, dating from the Neolithic and Bronze Age. The name Sannox is believed to have Viking origins and the area remained well-settled with numerous clachans and shielings. The Congregational Church was built in 1822, but the area was cleared of much of its population a few years later. It is known that many of them settled in Megantic County in Canada. The only real industry was a small barytes mine, which was opened in Glen Sannox in 1840. In 1862 the 11th Duke of Hamilton closed it as it was becoming an eyesore, but it reopened during the Great War and finally closed when it was exhausted in 1938. It had its own little railway running to a pier, but this was removed, leaving only the ruins of a few buildings.

Sannox has only a small range of features and facilities, including: the Gowanlea Guest House, Sannox Bay Hotel and restaurant, car park and toilets, Corrie Golf Club and tearoom.

WALK 38
North Glen Sannox Horseshoe

Distance	11km (6.5 miles)
Height gain	950m/3115ft
Start/finish	North Glen Sannox Bridge – grid ref. 993467
Terrain	Boggy and rocky at first, then later involving some exposed and arduous scrambling.
Refreshments	None closer than Sannox.

There is a fine horseshoe walk around North Glen Sannox, though the initial part of the walk crosses boggy, forested ground on the floor of the glen. After a rugged climb onto Sail an Im, the route climbs high around the 'dress circle' ridge to reach the summit of Caisteal Abhail. This much is fairly straightforward, but the continuation involves crossing the notorious cleft of Ceum na Caillich, or the Witch's Step, calling for a good head for heights and scrambling skills. In poor weather routes involving the Witch's Step are best avoided, and in really bad weather walkers would be well advised to retrace steps or head north from Caisteal Abhail down the rugged ridge between Garbh Coire and Coire nan Ceum for a safer descent.

There is a car park beside a bridge in **North Glen Sannox**, where a riverside path runs alongside **North Sannox Burn**. Note the fine waterfall pouring beneath the bridge, before following the path flanked by grass, heather and bog myrtle. A couple of small burns need to be forded, then there is a **tall gate** in a deer fence. The path is wet and muddy as it runs between a stand of forest and the river, passing many fine **waterfalls** as it climbs. There is a **ladder stile** leaving the top edge of the forest and the path continues upstream, with fine views of Caisteal Abhail and the rocky cleft of Ceum na Caillich, or the Witch's Step.

Leave the path by fording **North Sannox Burn** at some convenient point, then continue uphill, drifting gradually away from the river. The rugged face of Sail an Im is ahead, and by keeping to its left-hand side a relatively easy ascent can be made. A **steep slope** of heather and boulders also features low

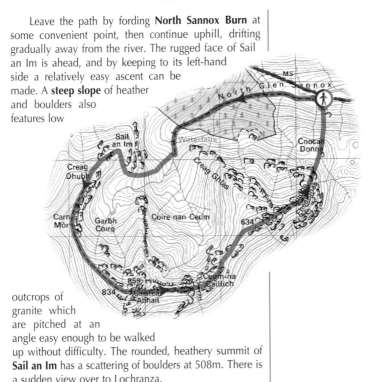

outcrops of granite which are pitched at an angle easy enough to be walked up without difficulty. The rounded, heathery summit of **Sail an Im** has a scattering of boulders at 508m. There is a sudden view over to Lochranza.

Turn left to pick up a **narrow path** which runs roughly south-west along the rounded ridge. The climb is on grass and heather, with some boulders and ribs of granite. Climb until a rounded granite hump is reached on top of the buttress of **Creag Dubh**, overlooking the Garbh Choire at 644m. Continue climbing at a fairly gentle gradient along the ridge, which levels out on **Carn Mòr** and gradually bends to the left as it rises towards Caisteal Abhail. ▶

The top of **Caisteal Abhail** features a handful of blocky granite tors which have the appearance of ruined castles. On a fine day they offer a host of interesting scrambling routes. The main summit is on one of these

Some walkers call this ridge the 'dress circle', and it offers splendid views in clear weather.

A final projecting slab of granite is an airy perch on the summit of Caisteal Abhail

tors, ending with a granite slab at 859m, which is easily gained. Views take in all the intricate details of Cir Mhòr and the ridges leading to Goat Fell and Cioch na h'Oighe. Further afield the rest of Arran is well displayed in its setting in the Clyde. Several portions of the mainland, Kintyre, Jura and Antrim can be seen.

Leave the summit of **Caisteal Abhail** by tracing a ridge path roughly eastwards. The path passes a couple of **blocky tors**, which adventurous walkers might like to scramble across. The path runs out onto a deceptively gentle, grassy shoulder, then drops down more ruggedly to a **bouldery gap**. Rising above this gap is a rocky, blocky **saw-tooth ridge**, which is best avoided by tracing a path across the Glen Sannox flank of the ridge. Just before reaching the Witch's Step, there is another bouldery tor furnishing a short scramble.

Crossing the **Witch's Step** calls for care and attention, a good head for heights and a willingness to use hands as well as feet. The descent into the gap is on **granite slabs**, which fall quite steeply. Always look for signs of previous passage, and use the available hand and foot holds. Don't drop down to any place without being confident that the move can be reversed. While the broad slabs can be unnerving, there are useful steps encountered on the final few steps down into the **gap**. ▶ Exit to the left of the gap, picking a way down a rather **worn gully**. Look to the right for a short scramble uphill, which shows obvious signs of use. A narrow path picks its way round a steep and rocky slope. There is another short scramble up some **jammed boulders**, then the path works its way back towards the main ridge.

The ridge is fairly narrow as it descends, and there is a good path cutting through the heather and crossing ribs of granite. A large **boulder** is passed before the next **gap** is reached. The path then climbs up a broader ridge featuring short grass, heather, low outcrops and boulders of granite. There is a minor summit to cross, followed by a little gap, then a worn and gritty path runs uphill onto **Suidhe Fhearghas**. This point is mostly rock with a little short grass and heather. There is a pointed block

The gap is a worn, yet sharp ridge. Towering above it is a steep and blocky granite peak which walkers will be pleased to hear that they don't need to climb.

Taking a break on the way down the steep and rocky slopes of Suidhe Fhearghas

projecting over Glen Sannox which makes the summit more easily identified in mist. The altitude is 660m and views take in the whole of Glen Sannox, with Beinn a' Chliabhain filling the deep gap of The Saddle.

The path runs plainly down the ridge in a series of **giant steps** separated by short level stretches. There are low outcrops and boulders amid the grass and heather, while areas of rotting granite make the path rather gritty. Towards the end of the ridge there is a spread of gritty ground followed by a broad, **low outcrop** of granite. Beyond that point there is a sudden steepening towards Sannox. The path swings to the left and runs steep and stony down a rugged slope. Note that there is a **slab of rock** to be crossed towards the foot of the slope. This can be avoided by taking action well in advance. Look out for a rowan tree in a **gully** and cut off to the left well above it, following a path which introduces a loop into the descent. This loop later swings right and runs beneath the slab.

There is a broad, boggy, heathery **gap** at the foot of this slope, where paths can be distinguished heading to left and right. The path heading left is rather vague, and it crosses the gap and keeps to the left of a couple of hummocky, heathery hills at **Cnocan Donna**. Looking over the edge in clear weather, the car park in **North Glen Sannox** can be seen beside the bridge. Closer to hand, and still below, the very tops of some **trees** can be seen. Keep to the right of these trees and walk down the heathery slope alongside. Heather gives way to bracken on the steep slope and a vague path runs straight down to the car park. A little squelchy ground is crossed before the **car park** and main road are reached.

WALK 39
Glen Sannox Horseshoe

Distance	16km (10 miles)
Height gain	1660m/5445ft
Start	Glen Cottage, Sannox – grid ref. 016454
Terrain	Rough mountain walking, with some clear paths on rocky ground. Serious rock scrambling is required in places.
Refreshments	Sannox Bay Hotel and Corrie Golf Club tearoom in Sannox.

The Glen Sannox Horseshoe offers a day of high adventure and the circuit is one of the Isle of Arran's mountain classics. Note at the outset that the route involves several rocky scrambles. The four most serious are the ascent of Cioch na h'Oighe, the descent from North Goat Fell, the ascent of Cir Mhòr and the traverse of Ceum na Caillich (The Witch's Step). Time will be lost at each of these points, especially when travelling as part of a group. The escape from The Saddle into Glen Sannox is itself a scramble down the steep and rocky Whin Dyke. In foul weather, the Glen Sannox Horseshoe should not be attempted, but in clear, dry weather competent, tough scramblers will find it a most entertaining round.

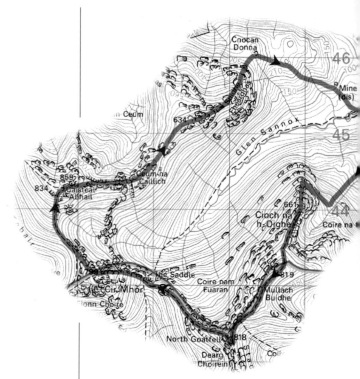

Start in between **Sannox** and Sannox Bridge, where there is roadside parking available near a riverside toilet block. Directly opposite the car park is **Glen Cottage** and a sign indicates the start of the cart track into Glen Sannox. Go through a tall gate and follow the narrow tarmac track uphill. It seems to head directly for Cioch na h'Oighe, but quickly bends to the right at a some small **burial grounds**. The track is rough and cobbly as it continues uphill and there is another **tall gate** to pass through. Tall white **marker posts** stand either side of the track, then there is a fine view around **Glen Sannox** which includes Cioch na h'Oighe, Cir Mhòr, Caisteal Abhail and Suidhe Fhearghas. The track climbs more gently, passing a small level green to the left, a footbridge and line of beech trees to the right. The ruins of **old mine buildings** are passed, then a rocky burn called the **Allt a' Chapuill** has to be forded in an area of spoil from an old barytes mine.

Turn left after fording the Allt a' Chapuill and follow a path upstream. This narrow path climbs up a rugged slope of grass, heather, bracken and bog myrtle. There are a series of small **waterfalls** in the burn, though these are sometimes obscured by birch trees which overhang the **rocky gorge**. When the last of the trees beside the burn are passed, the path and burn swing to the right. The path runs across a squelchy bowl of **moorland**, aiming more directly towards Cioch na h'Oighe. This more level stretch is followed by a steeper, bouldery, heathery slope; still with a trodden path. Again there are **waterfalls** along the course of the Allt a' Chapuill, and the flow seems more substantial at this point.

Don't follow the Allt a' Chapuill all the way up into **Coire na Ciche**, but cut off to the right across a slope of heather and boulders. The aim is to pick up the course of a narrow, gravelly path which slices across the **middle** of Cioch na h'Oighe. The path is quite clear at close quarters, but it is difficult to spot from below, and might be missed altogether by walkers who climb too high. Follow the narrow path across the steep slope, which has no real difficulties. The path turns a corner and has a view into Glen Sannox, but it is important not to be drawn into the glen. Instead, look out for a clear, narrow path which starts zigzagging steeply uphill to the left. This path climbs up to a **sloping face** of rock, and appears to terminate. Looking upwards, there appears to be a difficult scramble ahead. Retrace steps for a few paces to locate the start of an easier **scramble**.

The rock is bare, but there are good hand and foot holds. The path continuing uphill is rather vague in places, but it is generally possible to gauge its continuation without too much difficulty. The course of the trodden path often zigzags and any scrambles up **rocky outcrops** tend to be short and fairly easy. In fact, there is nothing as difficult as the first scramble at the start of this steep climb. The path later begins to move across the slope, so that views at one point overlook Glen Sannox, then later they overlook Coire na Ciche. After the final scramble the summit of **Cioch na h'Oighe** is revealed as a bare hump of granite at 661m, and there are awesomely rocky views ahead around Glen Sannox.

Don't be tempted to walk off **Cioch na h'Oighe** in the direction of a roller-coaster ridge, as there is overhanging rock projecting over the ridge. Instead, leave the summit of Cioch na h'Oighe as if dropping directly into Glen Sannox. A **path** can be joined which, by turning left, leads down to a little gap in the roller-coaster **ridge**. Climb uphill, following the path and a rocky scramble onto the narrow, rocky crest of the ridge. Walk carefully along the ridge, cutting off to the right where the path drops down to the next **gap** and avoids a **rock-step**.

Climb onto the next hump on the ridge, noting a small, creeping juniper on the way. The next two **notches** in the ridge are linked by a path, which picks its way across the flank overlooking Glen Sannox. Both notches feature strange upstanding spikes of granite. Continue along the

The tiny shape of a walker stands on Cioche na h'Oighe, the 'maiden's breast'

rocky crest, crossing the **highest part** of the roller-coaster ridge. Follow a well-worn path across a **broad gap**. The path climbs up to some **blocky slabs** on the flanks of Mullach Buidhe, then continues up a slope littered with large, low boulders. The path easily picks a way uphill between the boulders, then there is an easier grassy slope at a higher level. A **broad crest** of grass and low boulders has a good path that continues all the way across Mullach Buidhe. There are a couple of jumbled rocky outcrops overlooking Glen Sannox, but a more ordered pyramidal outcrop is the highest point on **Mullach Buidhe** at 830m.

There is a clear view ahead around Glen Sannox and towards Goat Fell. The ridge path runs down past embedded boulders to reach a **gap** below North Goat Fell. There are two paths ahead. The one to the right is used to reach the summit of North Goat Fell. The steep path climbs up a grassy slope, passing rocks to reach the crest of the fell. Turn left to reach the summit of bare granite on top of **North Goat Fell** at 818m.

Descending from North Goat Fell to The Saddle requires care. First drop down a chaotic arrangement of boulders, then walk down to cross an **exposed step**. Head down some rotten ribs and grooves of granite, where there is some security to be gained from wedging the body in the grooves. A buttress ahead has a curious **rocky projection** on the Glen Sannox side, but pass it on the Glen Rosa side to continue downhill. There are areas of rotten granite where gritty material is strewn across the slopes. Follow a worn path onto a bouldery ridge where there are few problems. There is a short, level, easy stretch on a heathery shoulder. Pick a way along a little **ledge** of rock overlooking Glen Sannox, then drop down a slope of clean granite. There is rotten, crumbling granite to cross before landing on the gap of **The Saddle** at 432m. Ahead are the awesome rocky slopes of Cir Mhòr.

Climbing uphill from **The Saddle** is relatively easy at first, where slopes of heather and granite slabs are pitched at a good gradient. The slope becomes steeper and trickier, with outcropping rock, slabs, boulders and. loose stones and grit. A brief, easier interlude follows along a **well-trodden path**. Above is the final part of the ascent, which needs great care. Very steep granite proves to be rotten and worn down to a treacherously bouldery and gritty condition. The boulders are sometimes jammed in heaps or wedged in gullies, but there are some loose specimens too. The nature of this ascent is always going to be subject to change and must always be approached with extreme caution. Every hand and foothold needs to be checked for stability. Above is the fine rock peak of **Cir Mhòr** at 799m.

Leave the summit by picking a way downhill carefully on rock and boulders. Look for traces of a path heading towards a **gap** on the way to Caisteal Abhail. The path is clearer on the final stages of the descent, crossing the gap and passing a **cairn**. Continue uphill, following the path along a blunt ridge and passing a couple more cairns. ◄ The main summit is on one of these tors, ending with a granite slab at 859m, which is easily gained and offers fine views.

The top of **Caisteal Abhail** features a handful of blocky granite tors, which have the appearance of ruined castles. On a fine day they offer a host of interesting scrambling routes.

Leave the summit of **Caisteal Abhail** by tracing a ridge path roughly eastwards. The path passes a couple of blocky **tors**, which adventurous walkers might like to scramble across. The path runs out onto a deceptively gentle, grassy shoulder, then drops down more ruggedly to a bouldery **gap**. Rising above this gap is a rocky, blocky **saw-tooth ridge**, which is best avoided by tracing a path across the Glen Sannox flank of the ridge. Just before reaching the Witch's Step, there is another bouldery tor furnishing a short scramble.

Crossing the **Witch's Step** calls for care and attention, a good head for heights and a willingness to use hands as well as feet.

◄ The descent into the gap is on **granite slabs**, which fall quite steeply. Always look for signs of previous passage, and use the available hand and foot holds. Don't drop down to any place without being confident that the move can be reversed. While the broad slabs can be unnerving, there are useful steps encountered on the final few steps down into the **gap**. The gap is a worn, yet sharp ridge. Towering above it is a steep and blocky granite peak which walkers will be pleased to hear that they don't need to climb. Exit to the left of the gap, picking a way down a rather **worn gully**. Look to the right

Cir Mhòr, Caisteal Abhail and the rocky ridge hiding the awkward Witch's Step

for a short scramble uphill, which shows obvious signs of use. A narrow path picks its way round a steep and rocky slope. There is another short scramble up some **jammed boulders**, then the path works its way back towards the main ridge.

The ridge is fairly narrow as it descends, and there is a good path cutting through the heather and crossing ribs of granite. A large **boulder** is passed before the next **gap** is reached. The path then climbs up a broader ridge featuring short grass, heather, low outcrops and boulders of granite. There is a minor summit to cross, followed by a little gap, then a worn and gritty path runs uphill onto **Suidhe Fhearghas**. This point is mostly rock with a little short grass and heather. There is a pointed block projecting over Glen Sannox which makes the summit more easily identified in mist. The altitude is 660m and views take in the whole of Glen Sannox, with Beinn a' Chliabhain filling the deep gap of The Saddle.

The path runs plainly down the ridge in a series of **giant steps** separated by short level stretches. There are low outcrops and boulders amid the grass and heather, while areas of rotting granite make the path rather gritty. Towards the end of the ridge there is a spread of gritty ground followed by a broad, **low outcrop** of granite. Beyond that point there is a sudden steepening towards Sannox. The path swings to the left and runs steep and stony down a rugged slope. Note that there is a **slab of**

211

rock to be crossed towards the foot of the slope. This can be avoided by taking action well in advance. Look out for a rowan tree in a **gully** and cut off to the left well above it, following a path which introduces a loop into the descent. This loop later swings right and runs beneath the slab.

There is a broad, boggy, heathery **gap** at the foot of this slope, where paths can be distinguished heading to left and right. The path to the right is fairly clear and it cuts across the heathery gap towards **Glen Sannox**. Follow the path down slopes of heather, crossing patches of bracken, to reach the lower grass and bracken slopes. Note the spoils of the **old barytes mines** and aim for the top of these. A broad mine incline track can be followed down towards **Sannox Burn**. Turn left around the corner of a tall **deer fence**, walking along a path through the bracken between the fence and the river. Cross over a wide wooden **bridge** and walk up to a track beside a stand of beech trees. Turn left to follow the **track** out of Glen Sannox, retracing the earliest steps of the day to reach the main road beside **Glen Cottage**.

WALK 40
Glen Sannox to Glen Rosa

Distance	16km (10 miles)
Height gain	450m/1475ft
Start	Glen Cottage, Sannox – grid ref. 016454
Finish	Ferry Terminal, Brodick – grid ref. 022359
Terrain	Easy walking on good paths through the glens. Scrambling is required over a gap in the mountains.
Refreshments	Sannox Bay Hotel and Corrie Golf Club tearoom in Sannox, Café Rosaburn at the Arran Heritage Museum, plenty of bars, cafés and restaurants around Brodick.

The walk from Glen Sannox to Glen Rosa is a popular route through the high mountains on the Isle of Arran. Being linear, it lends itself to being completed with the aid of bus services. Use the bus to reach Glen Sannox at the start of the day, and then walk back through the glens at your leisure to Brodick. There are good paths in the glens, though in recent years they were badly over-trodden and required reconstruction. The climb out of Glen Sannox is a rocky scramble up through the leaning gully of the Whin Dyke. The Saddle is slung between some of the highest mountains on the island, but on this walk it is a simple matter to head down through Glen Rosa. When the main road is reached, a bus might be caught back to Brodick, but in any case it takes little extra time to walk there.

Start in between **Sannox** and Sannox Bridge, where there is roadside parking available near a riverside toilet block. Directly opposite the car park is **Glen Cottage** and a sign indicates the start of the cart track into Glen Sannox. Go through a tall gate and follow the narrow tarmac track uphill. It seems to head directly for Cioch na h'Oighe, but quickly bends to the right at a some small **burial grounds**. The track is rough and cobbly as it continues uphill and there is another **tall gate** to pass through. Tall white **marker posts** stand either side of the track, then there is a fine view around Glen Sannox which includes Cioch na h'Oighe, Cir Mhòr, Caisteal

Map continues p.214

213

Abhail and Suidhe Fhearghas. The track climbs more gently, passing a small level green to the left, with a **footbridge** and line of beech trees to the right. Turn right to cross the wide, wooden footbridge, then turn left to follow a path beside **Sannox Burn**.

The path running along the length of **Glen Sannox** is usually firm, dry and practically level, though the ground to either side can be rugged and boggy. Enjoy the feeling of moving further and further towards the wild head of the glen, where high mountains tower on all sides. The lowest gap seen in the mountains ahead is The Saddle, and the **path** climbs towards it. Much of the path has been reconstructed and is plain and obvious to follow, fording **little burns** at the head of the glen, then climbing more and more steeply.

As height is gained, the path swings to the right and enters a steep, sloping, rocky gully, known as the **Whin Dyke**. The ascent is an awkward scramble at times, requiring care and the use of hands. Take greater care towards the top, where the ground is crumbling in places and the slope is quite steep. Also watch carefully as the path heads off to the left to reach **The Saddle** at 432m. There are granite slabs and outcrops in all directions, while slopes rising on either side of the gap are very steep and rugged. To the west is the formidable Cir Mhòr, while to the south-east is North Goat Fell.

The descent from The Saddle into **Glen Rosa** lies along a remarkably gentle path, descending at an easy gradient. Looking to the right, there is a fine view of the intricacies of the A' Chir ridge, should a traverse along it ever be contemplated. Walk down a bouldery, heathery tongue, fording a small **burn**. Follow the path easily through another bouldery, heathery area at a

Map continues p.216

The bouldery Glenrosa Water is full of small waterfalls and interesting rapids

gentler gradient, then drift more towards the course of **Glenrosa Water**. The river is often observed sliding across slabs of granite as it drains through the glen.

Keep to the path, whose surface is usually firm and dry, though the ground to either side is usually wet and boggy. The path follows the river downstream and passes a **large boulder** of granite. Look out for an attractive **waterfall**, which plunges into a deep pool in a rocky gorge overhung by birch trees. The path moves away from Glenrosa Water and crosses a wide wooden foot-bridge over the **Garbh Allt**, which is full of little waterfalls. From this point, it is simply a matter of following a clear and obvious **track** leading out of **Glen Rosa**. There is a gate along the way, and a **campsite** down to the left beside the river. Go through another gate and follow a narrow minor road past a few houses and farms to reach a junction with **The String road**.

Turn left along The String road, then right along the nearby main road for Brodick. This passes the **Arran Heritage Museum** and Brodick Primary School. It runs alongside the **Brodick Golf Course** and continues along the sea front all the way to the **ferry terminal**. For a list of features and facilities along the road through Brodick, see Walk 1.

WALK 41
Corrie and Goat Fell

Distance	15km (9.5 miles)
Height gain	1040m/3410ft
Start/finish	Glen Cottage, Sannox – grid ref. 016454
Terrain	Mostly on well-trodden paths, but some exposed scrambling on rock in places.
Refreshments	Sannox Bay Hotel and Corrie Golf Club tearoom at Sannox, Corrie Hotel at Corrie.

There is a rugged, entertaining horseshoe route climbing high above the villages of Sannox and Corrie. It embraces the summits of Cioch na h'Oighe, Mullach Buidhe, North Goat Fell and Goat Fell. The initial climb involves short rock scrambles and there is also an airy rock ridge to be followed. The route is not recommended in wintry or windy conditions, and in mist care is needed with navigation. There are easy escapes from the higher parts of the route, but on the ascent of Cioch na h'Oighe it is necessary to stick strictly to the route described. Short-cutting is asking for trouble and early descents are inadvisable before Mullach Buidhe. In clear weather, there is a chance to get to grips with the granite and enjoy amazing views into the rocky heart of northern Arran. The route described ends with a short road walk between Corrie and Sannox. This could be completed at the start of the walk, the end of the walk, or omitted entirely by catching a convenient bus between the two villages.

Start in between **Sannox** and Sannox Bridge, where there is roadside parking available near a riverside toilet block. Directly opposite the car park is **Glen Cottage** and a sign indicates the start of the cart track into Glen Sannox. Go through a tall gate and follow the narrow tarmac track uphill. It seems to head directly for Cioch na h'Oighe, but quickly bends to the right at a some small **burial grounds**. The track is rough and cobbly as it continues uphill and

there is another **tall gate** to pass through. Tall white **marker posts** stand either side of the track, then there is a fine view around **Glen Sannox** which includes Cioch na h'Oighe, Cir Mhòr, Caisteal Abhail and Suidhe Fhearghas. The track climbs more gently, passing a small level green to the left, a footbridge and line of beech trees to the right. The ruins of **old mine buildings** are passed, then a rocky burn called the **Allt a' Chapuill** has to be forded in an area of spoil from an old barytes mine.

Turn left after fording the Allt a' Chapuill and follow a path upstream. This narrow path climbs up a rugged slope of grass, heather, bracken and bog myrtle. There are a series of small **waterfalls** in the burn, though these are sometimes obscured by birch trees which overhang the **rocky gorge**. When the last of the trees beside the burn are passed, the path and burn swing to the right. The path runs across a squelchy bowl of **moorland**, aiming more directly towards Cioch na h'Oighe. This more level stretch is followed by a steeper, bouldery, heathery slope – still with a trodden path. Again there are **waterfalls** along the course of the Allt a' Chapuill, and the flow seems more substantial at this point.

Don't follow the Allt a' Chapuill all the way up into **Coire na Ciche**, but cut off to the right across a slope of heather and boulders. The aim is to pick up the course of a narrow, gravelly path which slices across the **middle** of Cioch na h'Oighe. The path is quite clear at close quarters, but it is difficult to spot from below, and might be missed altogether by walkers who climb too high. Follow the narrow path across the steep slope, which has no real difficulties. The path turns a corner and has a view into Glen Sannox, but it is important not to be drawn into the glen. Instead, look out for a clear, narrow path which starts zigzagging steeply uphill to the left. This path climbs up to a **sloping face** of rock, and appears to terminate. Looking upwards, there appears to be a difficult scramble ahead. Retrace steps for a few paces to locate the start of an easier **scramble**.

The rock is bare, but there are good hand and foot holds. The path continuing uphill is rather vague in places, but it is generally possible to gauge its continuation without too much difficulty. The course of the trodden path often zigzags and any scrambles up **rocky outcrops** tend to be short and fairly easy. In fact, there is nothing as difficult as the first scramble at the start of this steep climb. The path later begins to move across the slope, so that views at one point overlook Glen Sannox, then later they overlook Coire na Ciche. After the final scramble the summit of **Cioch na h'Oighe** is revealed as a bare hump of granite at 661m, and there are awesomely rocky views ahead around Glen Sannox.

Don't be tempted to walk off **Cioch na h'Oighe** in the direction of a roller-coaster ridge, as there is overhanging rock projecting over the ridge. Instead, leave the summit of Cioch na h'Oighe as if dropping directly into Glen Sannox. A **path** can be joined which, by turning left, leads down to a little gap in the roller-coaster **ridge**. Climb uphill, following the path and a rocky scramble onto the narrow, rocky crest of the ridge. Walk carefully along the ridge, cutting off to the right where the path drops down to the next **gap** and avoids a **rock-step**.

Climb onto the next hump on the ridge, noting a small, creeping juniper on the way. The next two **notches** in the ridge are linked by a path, which picks its way across the flank overlooking Glen Sannox. Both notches feature strange upstanding spikes of granite. Continue along the rocky crest, crossing the **highest part** of the roller-coaster ridge. Follow a well-worn path across a **broad gap**. The path climbs up to some **blocky slabs** on the flanks of Mullach Buidhe, then continues up a slope littered with large, low boulders. The path easily picks a way uphill between the boulders, then there is an easier grassy slope at a higher level. A **broad crest** of grass and low boulders has a good path that continues all the way across Mullach Buidhe. There are a couple of jumbled rocky outcrops overlooking Glen Sannox, but a more ordered pyramidal outcrop is the highest point on **Mullach Buidhe** at 830m.

There is a clear view ahead around Glen Sannox and towards Goat Fell. The ridge path runs down past embedded boulders to reach a **gap** below North Goat Fell. There are two paths ahead. The one to the right is used to reach the summit of North Goat Fell. The steep path climbs up a grassy slope, passing rocks to reach the crest of the fell. Turn left to reach the summit of bare granite on top of **North Goat Fell** at 818m.

To leave the summit of North Goat Fell, follow the narrow, blocky ridge onwards, stepping down from the rock to gain an easy path that crosses a **grassy gap** at 760m. Rising above the gap is a pyramidal tor of wrinkled granite, on the **Stacach Ridge**, where three options

Looking along the rugged ridge from Mullach Buidhe towards North Goat Fell

are available. One route is an almost direct ascent, to the left of some large, **jammed boulders**. A less direct route uses **giant steps** to the right of the boulders. Both these options are exposed scrambles. Walkers can also head round the **base** of the pyramid on the left side, overlooking the sea. Anyone climbing over the top of the tor will need to scramble down the other side. There are a couple more rocky bosses to scramble over if required. Anyone on the lower path can avoid all the rocky parts of the ridge by staying always on the seaward side of the ridge. A fourth route on the Glen Rosa flank might also be considered, though this is quite badly eroded.

The last part of the ridge is mostly a jumble of boulders through which the path continues towards Goat Fell. The summit of **Goat Fell** is a table of granite bearing a few large boulders, a trig point and a view indicator; the latter provided by the Rotary Club of Kilwinning. Goat Fell is the highest summit on the Isle of Arran at 874m, and views are naturally extensive and stretch far into mainland Scotland as well as embracing the Highlands, islands and Northern Ireland.

To leave the summit, follow the **ridge path** eastwards. The ground is bouldery, and the path is quite rugged as it weaves between boulders and blocky outcrops. There is a more level shoulder on **Meall Breac**, where the main path down to Brodick heads off to the right. However, keep straight on along the broad and bouldery crest, then descend a bouldery, heathery slope, where the path can be patchy in places and a couple of steps down may require the use of hands. Watch for the path drifting off to the left, down towards **Corrie Burn**.

The rough path fords Corrie Burn among a jumble of boulders, and should present no problems except in times of severe flooding. Turn right to continue downhill using a **reconstructed path** running parallel to the burn. The path leads down to a ladder stile over a tall **deer fence**. The continuation downhill is rather rough and bouldery in places. There is a **tall gate** in another deer fence, then the path runs downhill not far from a stand of **forest**.

A clear **track** is joined and the route continues downhill, passing a small **covered reservoir**. A narrow tarmac road runs down to the main coastal road on the outskirts of the village of **Corrie**. If attempting this route in reverse, this road is signposted for Goat Fell. Turn left to walk through the village along the main road. There may be a chance to obtain food or drink at the **Corrie Hotel**, or catch a bus in either direction.

CORRIE

A 'runrig' farm was recorded in Corrie in 1449, and by 1773 it was divided into three farms. In addition to farming there were quarries above the village, providing cut stone and lime. There was some decline in the population during the clearances around 1830, but there were enough people remaining for churches and a school to be built. The Free Church, now closed, dates from 1848. The 11th Duke of Hamilton provided a school in 1870, while the parish church dates from 1886. There was once a Congregational Church too. Corrie has a number of features and facilities which, listed from south to north include: Corrie and Sannox Village Hall and surgery, car park, harbour, toilets, then a long row of houses. Next comes North High Corrie Croft Bunk House, Corrie village shop, a couple of craft shops and the Corrie Hotel. Further on, beyond another long row of houses, is another harbour with a war memorial, yet another harbour, the parish church and Corrie Primary School.

Those who wish to walk back to Sannox should head all the way through Corrie, passing a bouldery and rocky shoreline with three small **harbours**. The long and straggly village ends with a huge **boulder** to the right of the road at **Clach a' Chath**. Cromwellian soldiers were slain in a battle at Clach a' Chath. Their bodies are said to have been buried at Lag nan Sasunnach near Sannox.

The coastal road features only occasional glimpses of the sea as it is quite well wooded, but look for seals hauled out on boulders, basking in the sun. There is a rugged, wooded cliff to the left, and a wooded raised beach to the right. Walking off the road proves to be very difficult and is not recommended. There is another huge

For a list of facilities in Sannox, see Walk 37.

boulder, this time to the left of the road, then after passing an outcrop of rough conglomerate rock, the village of **Sannox** is reached. Follow the road straight through to return to the small car park opposite **Glen Cottage**, where the walk started. ◄

WALK 42
Glen Rosa and Beinn Tarsuinn

Distance	15km (9.5 miles)
Height gain	1000m/3280ft
Start/finish	Glen Rosa Campsite – grid ref. 002376
Terrain	Rough mountain walking, with some clear paths on boggy or rocky ground.
Refreshments	None closer than Brodick.

There is an interesting little horseshoe circuit around Coire a' Bhradain on the western side of Glen Rosa. It could be completed as a circuit in its own right, or it could be used by walkers who set out on the Glen Rosa Horseshoe walk and realise that they are not going to be able to complete the full round. Beinn Nuis, Beinn Tarsuinn and Beinn a' Chliabhain form the 'nails' in the horseshoe, and an impressive traverse around the head of Coire Daingean is also included. A couple of sections of the Garbh Allt have been surrounded by tall deer fences to prevent sheep and deer from grazing. The intention is to enable the scanty tree cover beside the burn to regenerate. The course of the path is facilitated with tall kissing gates.

This walk starts from the Glen Rosa Campsite. To reach the campsite from Brodick, follow the main coastal road out of town, then turn left along the Blackwaterfoot road. Turn right almost immediately along the narrow minor road signposted as the cart track for Glen Rosa. If using bus serv-

Precipitous cliffs fall from the summit of Beinn Nuis into Coire a' Bhradain

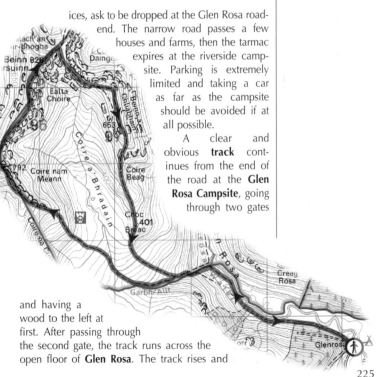

ices, ask to be dropped at the Glen Rosa road-end. The narrow road passes a few houses and farms, then the tarmac expires at the riverside campsite. Parking is extremely limited and taking a car as far as the campsite should be avoided if at all possible.

A clear and obvious **track** continues from the end of the road at the **Glen Rosa Campsite**, going through two gates and having a wood to the left at first. After passing through the second gate, the track runs across the open floor of **Glen Rosa**. The track rises and falls, twists and turns, but is generally firm, stony and dry underfoot. Cross a wide wooden **footbridge** and admire the waterfalls tumbling down the **Garbh Allt**. There are also fine views of the pyramidal peak of Cir Mhòr which dominates the head of Glen Rosa, and the pinnacles either side of Ceum na Caillich – the Witch's Step – which are actually over in neighbouring Glen Sannox.

After crossing the **footbridge**, turn left and pick up the path which runs uphill roughly parallel to the waters of the **Garbh Allt**. Patches of bog myrtle near the bridge give way to bracken and heather cover as height is gained on the steep and bouldery slope. A fenced enclosure is entered at a **kissing gate**, then the path climbs uphill. The path is rather rough, but offers better walking than the tussocks of grass alongside. There are many small **waterfalls** in the Garbh Allt and a small dam might be noticed where water was once collected and piped down through Glen Rosa. Another **kissing gate** is passed and the path continues beside the burn. The waterfalls often roar down rocky slopes, while at a higher level the path runs across a gentler **moorland shoulder** and the river runs through a small rocky gorge.

Go through a **kissing gate** to enter another fenced enclosure surrounding the gorge. There are views around the fine little horseshoe of peaks encircling **Coire a' Bhradain**. Look out for a narrow little path crossing the gorge and fording the burn. In very wet weather it might be inadvisable to cross. Another **kissing gate** allows an exit from the fenced enclosure, then the path climbs towards mountains. ◀

The **path** heads away from the burn and crosses a soggy moorland slope before climbing more steeply. After passing small slabs of granite, the path drifts to the right and follows a rib of granite. The way uphill is usually clearly trodden, except where the route crosses slabs of granite. These **outcrops** are set at an easy angle. Looking across the gap between Beinn Tarsuinn and Beinn a' Chliabhain, the peaks of A' Chir and Cir Mhòr can be seen.

There is a less rocky shoulder to climb and the **path** is very clear, having been reconstructed after the grass

The rocky ridge ahead, which features the pyramidal form of Beinn Nuis to the left, followed by Beinn Tarsuinn in the middle and Beinn a' Chliabhain to the far right. The summit of Goat Fell, which has been visible throughout the ascent, remains in view over a shoulder of Beinn a' Chliabhain.

and heather slopes suffered erosion. It threads its way past low, rounded tors and boulders, before a final pull up to the summit of **Beinn Nuis**. Large boulders of granite protrude from the 792m summit and there is a small cairn. Views encompass Glen Rosa, with a peep through to Glen Sannox over the gap of The Saddle. Southern Arran is well displayed, but has few significant features. The Pirnmill Hills rise in a mountainous barrier beyond Loch Tanna.

A path descends from the summit of **Beinn Nuis**, picking its way down a steep and bouldery slope to a **gap** before continuing along the high ridge. There are fine views of rocky buttresses overlooking Glen Rosa, then the path runs along the side of the ridge overlooking Glen Iorsa to avoid a bouldery scramble. On the next uphill stretch there is a tremendous view along the length of Glen Iorsa, featuring its little loch towards the sea, its awesomely boggy stretches along its floor, and the meandering course of its river. Walking uphill, there are many large, rounded, boulders to be passed. The ridge broadens and is clothed in short grass and moss, then it narrows and rises again. Just before a dip in the ridge the **Old Man of Tarsuinn** presents a sort of human profile off to the right.

OLD MAN OF TARSUINN

The Old Man of Tarsuinn is a comical natural sculpture projecting from the ridge between Beinn Nuis and Beinn Tarsuinn. Its profile resembles that of Popeye, or some other gnarled seafarer, and appropriately the figure appears to gaze out to sea. After a couple of visits, walkers should be able to spot the Old Man even from distant Brodick, even though it is a mere pimple on the rocky ridge.

Cross the dip and climb a final, short, bouldery slope to reach the summit of **Beinn Tarsuinn** at 826m. There are twin summits with no real difference between them; each have low outcrops and boulders of granite. Views ahead tend to make A' Chir merge into Cir Mhòr, but it is important to remember that these two peaks are quite separate and that there is no walking route directly from one to the other.

A path runs steeply downhill from **Beinn Tarsuinn** and there is a need to grapple with some big boulders and outcrops of granite. Sometimes there is a choice of paths, and at one point there is even the option of walking beneath a **huge boulder**. After much squeezing and slithering the bottom of the slope is reached and the gap of **Bealach an Fhir-bhogha** is gained. From certain points on the gap it is possible to see the pyramidal form of Ailsa Craig and the humps of the Paps of Jura, both out to sea in the distance, but in opposite directions.

To leave **Bealach an Fhir-bhogha**, turn sharply to the right to spot a path which contours beneath a monstrous granite face overlooking **Coire Daingean** and Glen Rosa. The path is narrow and clings to a steep slope, but it is continuous throughout. Looking upwards, tottering blocks of granite can be seen, and there is a long, dark slit slicing through the rock face. The path runs downhill on a crumbly slope, then rises to gain the **crest of the ridge** between Beinn Tarsuinn and Beinn a' Chliabhain. Throughout the traverse, there are fine views into Glen Rosa.

Turn left along the rocky crest, following a path that soon crosses a gentle, **grassy gap**. Note that the path proceeds by cutting across the western slopes of Beinn a' Chliabhain. If a summit bid is to be made, then it is necessary to start climbing to the left to stay on the ridge. Grass, heather and boulders give way to a fine rocky ridge. The summit of **Beinn a' Chliabhain** rises to 653m and offers fine views around Glen Rosa from an airy perch. There is a last chance to sample the distant views too, which stretch from Antrim to Galloway and Ayrshire and include Ailsa Craig and Holy Isle.

Continue along the **ridge path**, which joins the path skirting along the flank of the mountain. The path is clear and stony, braided in places, running down a broadening, bouldery, moorland slope. The gradient eases later, where boggy ground and granite slabs are followed by a bouldery **cairn**. Continue to trace the path downhill, though it is rather less clear on the broad, boggy slopes of tussocky grass. The path swings to the left as it approaches the Garbh Allt, and it reaches a **kissing gate** at the corner of a fenced enclosure.

All that remains is to retrace the earlier steps of the day. Follow the steep and rugged path downhill alongside the waterfalls of the **Garbh Allt** and pass through another **kissing gate** at the bottom of the fenced enclosure. Turn right to cross the **footbridge** over the Garbh Allt, then follow the clear track through **Glen Rosa** to return to the campsite. Continue along the road if returning to **Brodick**.

Looking from Beinn a' Chliabhain towards A' Chir, Caisteal Abhail and Cir Mhòr

WALK 43
Western Glen Rosa

Distance	19km (12 miles)
Height gain	1250m/4100ft
Start/finish	Glen Rosa Campsite – grid ref. 002376
Terrain	Rough mountain walking, with some clear paths on boggy or rocky ground. Some rock scrambling is required in places.
Refreshments	None closer than Brodick.

Tough walkers who are prepared to start early and finish late on a good, clear day would just about be able to manage the long walk around the Glen Rosa Horseshoe. Other walkers will need to tackle the round in two halves. The western half is the toughest, requiring a long ascent, some steep and rugged slopes, and even some scrambling on steep rock at times. The wrinkly rock faces of A' Chir are beyond the capabilities of more cautious walkers, and it is true that the full traverse of the rocky ridge is really the domain of rock climbers. Walkers who wish to bring the summit of A' Chir underfoot should refer to the separate short route description at the end of this section. There is a campsite on the way into Glen Rosa, and camping there gives walkers a head start on this route. Those who drive into the glen could have difficulty securing a parking space and buses do not use the minor road. Many walkers are prepared to cover the road-walk from Brodick to Glen Rosa, though it costs extra in terms of time, distance and effort.

This walk starts from the Glen Rosa Campsite. To reach the campsite from Brodick, follow the main coastal road out of town, then turn left along the Blackwaterfoot road. Turn right almost immediately along the narrow minor road signposted as the cart track for Glen Rosa. If using buses, ask to be dropped at the Glen Rosa road-end. The narrow road passes a few houses and farms, then the

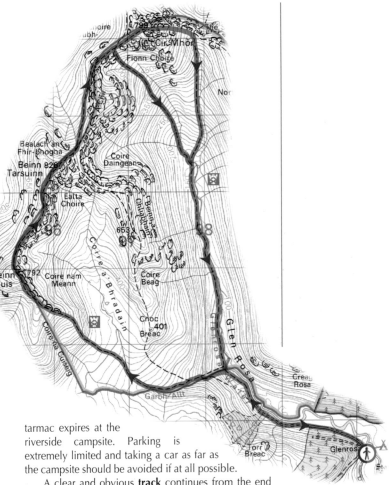

tarmac expires at the riverside campsite. Parking is extremely limited and taking a car as far as the campsite should be avoided if at all possible.

A clear and obvious **track** continues from the end of the road at the **Glen Rosa Campsite**, going through two gates and having a wood to the left at first. After passing through the second gate, the track runs across the open floor of **Glen Rosa**. The track rises and falls, twists and turns, but is generally firm, stony and dry underfoot.

Cross a wide wooden **footbridge** and admire the water-falls tumbling down the **Garbh Allt**. There are also fine views of the pyramidal peak of Cir Mhòr which dominates the head of Glen Rosa, and the pinnacles either side of Ceum na Caillich – the Witch's Step – which are actually over in neighbouring Glen Sannox.

After crossing the **footbridge**, turn left and pick up the path which runs uphill roughly parallel to the waters of the **Garbh Allt**. Patches of bog myrtle near the bridge give way to bracken and heather cover as height is gained on the steep and bouldery slope. A fenced enclosure is entered at a **kissing gate**, then the path climbs uphill. The path is rather rough, but offers better walking than the tussocks of grass alongside. There are many small **waterfalls** in the Garbh Allt and a small dam might be noticed where water was once collected and piped down through Glen Rosa. Another **kissing gate** is passed and the path continues beside the burn. The waterfalls often roar down rocky slopes, while at a higher level the path runs across a gentler **moorland shoulder** and the river runs through a small rocky gorge.

Go through a **kissing gate** to enter another fenced enclosure surrounding the gorge. There are views around the fine little horseshoe of peaks encircling **Coire a' Bhradain**. Look out for a narrow little path crossing the gorge and fording the burn. In very wet weather it might be inadvisable to cross. Another **kissing gate** allows an exit from the fenced enclosure, then the path climbs towards mountains. Study the rocky ridge ahead, which features the pyramidal form of Beinn Nuis to the left, followed by Beinn Tarsuinn in the middle and Beinn a' Chliabhain to the far right. The summit of Goat Fell, which has been visible throughout the ascent, remains in view over a shoulder of Beinn a' Chliabhain.

The **path** heads away from the burn and crosses a soggy moorland slope before climbing more steeply. After passing small slabs of granite, the path drifts to the right and follows a rib of granite. The way uphill is usually clearly trodden, except where the route crosses slabs of granite. These **outcrops** are set at an easy angle. Looking across the gap between Beinn Tarsuinn and Beinn a' Chliabhain, the peaks of A' Chir and Cir Mhòr can be seen.

There is a less rocky shoulder to climb and the **path** is very clear, having been reconstructed after the grass and heather slopes suffered erosion. It threads its way past low, rounded tors and boulders, before a final pull up to the summit of **Beinn Nuis**. Large boulders of granite protrude from the 792m summit and there is a small cairn. Views encompass Glen Rosa, with a peep through to Glen Sannox over the gap of The Saddle. Southern Arran is well displayed, but has few significant features. The Pirnmill Hills rise in a mountainous barrier beyond Loch Tanna.

A path descends from the summit of **Beinn Nuis**, picking its way down a steep and bouldery slope to a **gap** before continuing along the high ridge. There are fine views of rocky buttresses overlooking Glen Rosa, then the path runs along the side of the ridge overlooking Glen Iorsa to avoid a bouldery scramble. ▶

Walking uphill, there are many large, rounded, boulders to be passed. The ridge broadens and is clothed in

On the next uphill stretch there is a tremendous view along the length of Glen Iorsa, featuring its little loch towards the sea, its awesomely boggy stretches along its floor, and the meandering course of its river.

The natural granite sculpture of the Old Man of Tarsuinn looks out over the glens

short grass and moss, then it narrows and rises again. Just before a dip in the ridge the **Old Man of Tarsuinn** presents a sort of human profile off to the right. Cross the dip and climb a final, short, bouldery slope to reach the summit of **Beinn Tarsuinn** (826m). There are twin summits with no real difference between them; each having low outcrops and boulders of granite. Views ahead tend to make A' Chir merge into Cir Mhòr, but it is important to remember that these two peaks are quite separate and that there is no walking route from one to the other. This will become apparent later.

A path runs steeply downhill from **Beinn Tarsuinn** and there is a need to grapple with some big boulders and outcrops of granite. Sometimes there is a choice of paths, and at one point there is even the option of walking beneath a **huge boulder**. After much squeezing and slithering the bottom of the slope is reached and the gap of **Bealach an Fhir-bhogha** is gained. From certain points on the gap it is possible to see the pyramidal form of Ailsa Craig and the humps of the Paps of Jura, both out to sea in the distance, but in opposite directions.

There are two paths leaving **Bealach an Fhir-bhogha**, a high-level and low-level path. The high-level path heads for the summit of **A' Chir** and walkers are referred to the separate route description below for details. Use the low-level path to continue with this particular walk, which avoids the A' Chir ridge.

The low-level path leads beneath the **boilerplate slabs** of granite which flank **A' Chir** on the Glen Iorsa side. The path is narrow in places, though it should always be distinguishable ahead. It dips downhill to pass beneath the foot of the slabs. This is something of a 'weeping wall' with clean granite slabs dripping or running with water, and only a few rugs or carpets of heather able to keep hold on the steep rock. The path rises from the base of the slabs and reaches a little **notch** in the ridge offering a view back along the more difficult parts of the A' Chir ridge. The path continues away from the summit in the direction of Cir Mhòr. There is a short **rock-step** giving access to an inclined table of rock on

The fine ridge between Cir Mhòr and Caisteal Abhail

the rugged crest of the ridge. The path runs down to a broad, bouldery **gap**, where a small cairn sits on the lowest part. Note that there is a useful escape path down to the right, into **Coire Buidhe**, if an ascent of Cir Mhòr is not required on this particular outing.

The path climbing Cir Mhòr starts by wriggling up a **bouldery slope**. At one point there is a short link to the left with the ridge path serving Castail Abhail. Be careful not to be drawn off-route in mist. The final part of **Cir Mhòr** rises even more steeply and the summit peak of rock is gained only by grappling with the last rocky rise. From the 799m stance there are amazing views around the ridges of Glen Rosa and Glen Sannox. The peaks of Goat Fell, Cioch na h'Oighe and Caisteal Abhail all feature prominently, as well as the A' Chir ridge which was so recently outflanked. The more distant Pirnmill Hills are seen across Glen Iorsa.

The descent from **Cir Mhòr** to The Saddle needs exceptional care. Looking down from the summit, only a couple of portions of the path near the top can be seen. What is not apparent is the nature of the terrain. **Very steep**

granite proves to be rotten and worn down to a treacherously bouldery and gritty condition. The boulders are
sometimes jammed in heaps or wedged in gullies, but
there are some loose specimens too. The nature of this
descent is always going to be subject to change and must
always be approached with extreme caution. The first part
of the descent is steep and horrible, with every hand and
foot hold needing to be checked for stability, then there is
a brief, easy interlude along a **well-trodden path**. Another
steep and rugged drop picks a way down a steep slope
where there is outcropping rock, slabs, boulders and loose
stones and grit. This steep and tricky slope continues all
the way down to **The Saddle** at 432m. Only on the final
parts of the descent are there any easy gradients, where
slopes of heather and slabs pitched at an easier angle lead
onto the gap. Anyone wishing to complete the full Glen
Rosa Horseshoe can switch to Walk 44 and pick up the
route description from **The Saddle**.

Alternative descent to Glen Rosa

Walkers who start to venture down towards The Saddle
and suddenly find themselves backing out in fear can try
an alternative descent towards Glen Rosa. Retrace steps
back over the top of **Cir Mhòr** and go down to the **gap**
between Cir Mhòr and A' Chir. A small cairn marks the
start of the path down into **Coire Buidhe**. The first part of
the path consists of steep, loose, stony material. Later,
there is a gentler path, before another drop leads down
through **Fionn Choire** into **Glen Rosa**.

The descent from The Saddle into **Glen Rosa** lies along a
remarkably gentle path, descending at an easy gradient.
Looking to the right, there is a fine view of the intricacies
of the A' Chir ridge, should a traverse along it ever be
contemplated. Continue down a bouldery, heathery
tongue, fording a small **burn**. Follow the path easily
through another bouldery, heathery area at a gentler
gradient, then drift more towards the course of **Glenrosa
Water**. The river is often observed sliding across slabs of
granite as it drains through the glen.

Keep to the path, whose surface is usually firm and dry, though the ground to either side is usually wet and boggy. The path follows the river downstream and passes a large **boulder** of granite. Look out for an attractive **waterfall**, which plunges into a deep pool in a rocky gorge overhung by birch trees. The path moves away from Glenrosa Water and crosses a wide wooden footbridge over the **Garbh Allt**, which is full of little waterfalls. From this point, it is simply a matter of retracing your earlier steps of the day along a clear and obvious **track** out of **Glen Rosa**. There is a gate along the way, and by the time tarmac is reached, the **Glen Rosa Campsite is** down to the left beside the river. Continue along the road if returning to **Brodick**.

GLEN ROSA

Facilities in Glen Rosa are limited to the Glen Rosa Campsite and a few self-catering cottages. Practically all of the Glen Rosa Horseshoe, and some land outside its bounds, is owned and managed by the National Trust for Scotland. The extent of their holdings in the mountains is around 7000 acres.

A' Chir

Those walkers who wish to include the summit of A' Chir in this walk should note that there is some steep and exposed scrambling even on the easiest ascent. Starting from **Bealach an Fhir-bhogha**, take the path running uphill. This stays on the Glen Iorsa side of the rugged ridge, then gains the crest of the ridge at a **notch** overlooked by a monstrous buttress of rock. Take a path to the left, then scramble up boulders and slabs. Another path at a higher level picks its way along a **narrow ledge** on a sloping boilerplate slab overlooking Glen Iorsa, then it gains the rocky crest and reaches another **notch**. It is possible to scramble down into the notch in a couple of places, but the rock can be damp and greasy, and a slip could have disastrous consequences. This awkward descent can be avoided by backtracking a little along the ridge, then dropping down to another **thin path** on the Glen Iorsa side. The path leads

While **experienced rock climbers** would be able to progress without the use of a rope, others should consider roping up for safety. A couple of experienced rock climbers using ropes might be able to get a couple more less accomplished climbers along the rest of the ridge.

along a **ledge**, which runs into a **gully** just below the **notch**. To the left of this gully is an exposed rock scramble on **sloping slabs**, allowing the crest to be regained. Once this has been accomplished, walk and scramble towards the summit of **A' Chir**, which is a monstrous perched boulder at 745m. Walkers may be excused for not tackling this final obstacle!

Continuing along the **A' Chir** ridge towards **Cir Mhòr** is fraught with difficulties and is actually graded as a rock climb. Anyone experiencing hardship scrambling to the summit of A' Chir would not be able to cover the rest of the ridge. ◄ **Cautious explorers** who have managed to reach the summit of **A' Chir**, but don't want to be drawn along the rest of the ridge should retrace steps faithfully to **Bealach an Fhir-bhogha**. If anything, the descent is rather trickier than the ascent and it certainly needs more care. The first full traverse of the A' Chir ridge was accomplished in January 1892.

WALK 44
Eastern Glen Rosa

Distance	18km (11 miles)
Height gain	950m/3115ft
Start/finish	Glen Rosa Campsite – grid ref. 002376
Terrain	Rugged paths throughout the ascent, with some short rocky scrambles. Easier road walking at the end.
Refreshments	None closer than Brodick

The Glen Rosa Horseshoe can be completed in a good, long, hard day's walk by tough and experienced hill walkers. Other walkers may prefer to tread more cautiously and complete the horseshoe walk in two easier halves. Note the use of the word 'easier' and not 'easy'. The Glen Rosa Horseshoe can never be easy and there are some very steep and exposed rocky slopes. Some basic scrambling is required in places. The western half of the horseshoe has some of the more arduous scrambles, while the eastern half is somewhat easier on the hands. The walk includes Goat Fell, which is the highest mountain on the Isle of Arran and offers the most extensive views. While the eastern half of the Glen Rosa Horseshoe can be conveniently started at the Glen Rosa Campsite, there is no transport along the dead-end road and parking for cars can be tight. A taxi ride from Brodick might be considered, though walkers who are prepared to camp in Glen Rosa can please themselves how and when to start the walk. Returning directly from Goat Fell to Glen Rosa at the end of the day can be difficult, so the route given to close the circuit is, although long, much easier. An alternative finish could be made at Brodick Castle or down on the main road nearby, if you can arrive in time for a bus.

This walk starts from the Glen Rosa Campsite. To reach the campsite from Brodick, follow the main coastal road out of town, then turn left along the Blackwaterfoot road. Turn right almost immediately along the narrow minor road signposted as the cart track for Glen Rosa. If using buses, ask to be dropped at the Glen Rosa road-end. The narrow road passes a few houses and farms, then the tarmac expires at the riverside campsite. Parking is extremely limited and taking a car as far as the campsite should be avoided if at all possible.

A clear and obvious **track** continues from the end of the road at the **Glen Rosa Campsite**, going through two gates and having a wood to the left at first. After passing through the second gate, the track runs across the open floor of **Glen Rosa**. The track rises and falls, twists and turns, but is generally firm, stony and dry underfoot. Cross a wide wooden **footbridge** and admire the waterfalls tumbling down the **Garbh Allt**. There are also fine views of the pyramidal peak of Cir Mhòr which dominates the head of Glen Rosa, and the pinnacles either side of Ceum na Caillich – the Witch's Step – which are actually over in neighbouring Glen Sannox.

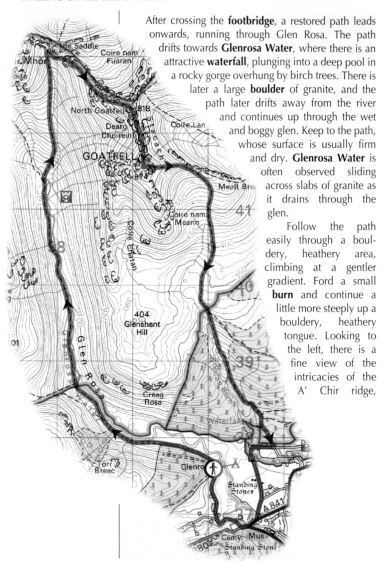

After crossing the **footbridge**, a restored path leads onwards, running through Glen Rosa. The path drifts towards **Glenrosa Water**, where there is an attractive **waterfall**, plunging into a deep pool in a rocky gorge overhung by birch trees. There is later a large **boulder** of granite, and the path later drifts away from the river and continues up through the wet and boggy glen. Keep to the path, whose surface is usually firm and dry. **Glenrosa Water** is often observed sliding across slabs of granite as it drains through the glen.

Follow the path easily through a bouldery, heathery area, climbing at a gentler gradient. Ford a small **burn** and continue a little more steeply up a bouldery, heathery tongue. Looking to the left, there is a fine view of the intricacies of the A' Chir ridge,

should a traverse along it ever be contemplated. The awesomely rugged Cir Mhòr completely dominates to the left of The Saddle, while North Goat Fell rises steeply to the right. The path is reasonably gentle all the way to **The Saddle** at 432m.

Steep and rocky ridges fall from North Goat Fell to The Saddle and Cir Mhòr

The Saddle sits amid low outcrops of granite, with a fine view over into **Glen Sannox**. Turn right to follow the path climbing towards North Goat Fell. This crosses the lowest part of the gap, which is strewn with grit and gravel. Clean, hard granite gives way to rotten, crumbling granite as the **ridge** is followed higher. More clean granite follows and there are splendid views back towards the peak of Cir Mhòr. There is one point where it is necessary to pick a way across a little **ledge** of rock overlooking Glen Sannox. Beyond is a short, level, easy stretch on a **heathery shoulder**. The path then climbs uphill on a bouldery ridge with no real difficulties for a while.

On a higher part of the ridge there is a worn **path** on a grassy slope, then more rock becomes apparent towards the top. The rock is rotten and gritty material has been washed down towards Glen Rosa. There is a buttress ahead which has a curious **rocky projection** on the Glen Sannox side. Pass the buttress on the Glen Rosa side and regain the crest of the ridge at a notch. Ribs and grooves of granite, although rotten, offer some security on an uphill scramble. There is an **exposed step** to negotiate before the next uphill pull. The final climb crosses a chaotic arrangement of boulders and reaches an inclined slab, which is the summit of **North Goat Fell** at 818m.

To leave North Goat Fell, follow the narrow, blocky ridge onwards, stepping down from the rock to gain an easy path that crosses a **grassy gap** at 760m. Rising above the gap is a pyramidal tor of wrinkled granite, on the **Stacach Ridge**, where three options are available. One route is an almost direct ascent, to the left of some large, **jammed boulders**. A less direct route uses **giant steps** to the right of the boulders. ◀ Walkers can also head round the **base** of the pyramid on the left side, overlooking the sea. Anyone climbing over the top of the tor will need to scramble down the other side. There are a couple more rocky bosses to scramble over if required. Anyone on the lower path can avoid all the rocky parts of the ridge by staying always on the seaward side of the ridge. A fourth route on the Glen Rosa flank might also be considered, though this is quite badly eroded.

The last part of the ridge is mostly a jumble of boulders through which the path continues towards Goat Fell. The summit of **Goat Fell** is a table of granite bearing a few large boulders, a trig point and a view indicator; the latter is provided by the Rotary Club of Kilwinning. Goat Fell is the highest summit on the Isle of Arran at 874m, and views are naturally extensive and stretches far into mainland Scotland as well as embracing the Highlands, islands and Northern Ireland.

To leave the summit, follow the **ridge path** eastwards. The ground is bouldery, and the path is quite rugged as it weaves between boulders and blocky outcrops. There is a more level shoulder on **Meall Breac**, at which point the main path heads off to the right. The line of the path has been restored and features pitched

Both these options are exposed scrambles.

stonework, drains and a good, firm surface. The surrounding moorland is mostly wet, grassy, heathery and bouldery. On some short stretches the path runs over **granite slabs**. A tall deer fence is reached and a **gate** gives access to a more rugged lower path. (Following the deer fence off to the right offers a rugged return to Glen Rosa, ending with a river crossing.) The path runs down a heathery slope and crosses a channel of water constructed across the hillside. Stands of **forest** lie some distance from the path, and the heather and bracken slope features a few areas of birch.

The path goes through an old **gateway** in a drystone wall, then goes through an area where rhododendron bushes have been cut back. Continue down through a crossroads of forest tracks, going straight onwards and straight downhill. At the next junction, turn right and continue downhill. Take no notice of **waymarks** pointing to left or right, but simply walk down the most obvious **track**. Looking back, some markers state that the track is leading to Goat Fell, and by the time a narrow **tarmac road** is reached there is an information board erected by the National Trust for Scotland.

The road could be followed to the left to reach **Brodick Castle**, though it may well be closed this late in the day. The track crosses the road and could be followed straight onwards down to **Cladach** and the main road, where there are bus services. Turning right along the narrow road, however, leads past a large house known as **The Kennels**. The road continues across a **bridge** in a wooded area, then runs downhill and through fields. Well-trimmed beech hedges obscure a view of three tall **standing stones:** one is to the left of the road and two are to the right. The road continues to a **gate lodge** where there is an exit onto the main road. Turn right and cross **Rosa Bridge**, then turn right again along the Blackwaterfoot road. A final right turn is signposted for **Glen Rosa**, running back to the campsite where the walk started.

WALK 45
The Arran Coastal Way

Distance	Up to 113km (70 miles) depending on the choice of route
Start/finish	Ferry Terminal, Brodick – grid ref. 022359
Terrain	Roads, tracks and paths, as well as sandy, pebbly and bouldery beach walks. A few sections need care at high water.
Refreshments	Bars, cafés and restaurants are available at regular intervals, including Brodick, Lamlash, Whiting Bay, Kildonan, Lagg, Blackwaterfoot, Machrie, Pirnmill, Catacol, Lochranza, Sannox, Corrie and Cladach.

This is not intended to be a detailed route description, but simply serves to highlight the fact that a complete coastal walk around the Isle of Arran is available. The route could be comfortably completed within a week, but bear in mind that it is not specifically signposted or waymarked, and in many instances there is no trodden path, only rocky, bouldery raised beaches. The emphasis is on adventurous exploration, and while most of the route is safe from high tides, there are one or two short stretches where high water could be a problem. A group of enthusiasts on the Isle of Arran are promoting the route to visiting walkers, and are always happy to offer help and advice. Walkers who want to treat the route as a long-distance walk can have their baggage transferred from place to place, and stay in hotels and bed and breakfasts. Those who wish to operate from a single base will find that there is always good access to the main road and its bus services.

The logical starting point for a walk around the coastline of the Isle of Arran is Brodick, even to the extent of stepping ashore from the ferry and starting the walk straight away. As many sections of the Arran Coastal Way are already covered in many of the walks in this guidebook, the route description offered here is in a simplified form. In many instances the main A841 road runs very close to

Looking across a placid Brodick Bay towards the towering peak of Goat Fell

the coast, so a route description is hardly necessary, and walkers can choose whether to follow it, or whether to walk closer to the shore.

Day 1: Brodick to Kildonan – 26km (16 miles)

Refer to Walk 3 and Walk 5 for the route from **Brodick**, through **Corriegills** and around **Clauchlands Point** to reach **Lamlash**. A side-trip by ferry from Lamlash to **Holy Isle**, as detailed in Walk 8, is to be commended but should be considered as an optional extra. To continue around **Lamlash Bay**, use the route in Walk 13 to reach **Kingscross Point** and **Whiting Bay**. Beyond Whiting Bay, the main road pulls away from the coast and the walk from **Largymore** around **Dippin Head** is very rough and rocky in places. However, the walk becomes much easier as it approaches the village of **Kildonan**.

Day 2: Kildonan to Blackwaterfoot – 22km (14 miles)

Refer to Walk 14 in reverse for a route from **Kildonan**, around **Bennan Head**, to the **Torrylin Cairn** and **Lagg**. Bear in mind that the tide has to be out before it is safe to pass the **Black Cave** at the foot of Bennan Head. Use the main road to walk from **Lagg**, through **Sliddery**, to **Corriecravie**. There is a signposted track to **Cleat's Shore**, which is the Isle of Arran's only official naturist beach. If this detour is not required, then the shore can be gained by following part of Walk 16 in reverse, from **Torr A' Chaisteal Dun** to the **Preaching Cave**, then continue along the shore to **Blackwaterfoot**.

Day 3: Blackwaterfoot to Pirnmill – 22km (14 miles)

Follow Walk 22 from **Blackwaterfoot** to the **Doon** and past the **King's Cave**. When the route reaches the main road, walk along the road through **Machrie**, and maybe consider a detour onto **Machrie Moor** as detailed in Walk 23. The main road is seldom far from the shore on the way to **Dougarie**, but there are interesting archaeological remains just inland, which can be inspected with

reference to Walk 24. Continue along the road, using the shore where possible, especially from **Imachar**, around **Imachar Point**, to pass the settlement of **Whitefarland**. The route reaches the village of **Pirnmill** shortly afterwards.

Looking around Machrie Bay to the Pirnmill Hills in the north-west of the island

Day 4: Pirnmill to Sannox – 26km (16 miles)

The road runs very close to the shore all the way from **Pirnmill**, through **Thundergay**, to the village of **Catacol**. There is an easy route, and even a fine grassy track, between Catacol and **Lochranza**, but there is also the option of using the **Postman's Path** over the clifftop, though this can be wet and muddy. Leaving Lochranza, refer to parts of Walk 35 and Walk 37 for a splendid coastal path around the **Cock of Arran** that is far removed from the road. The route passes the isolated cottage of **Laggan** and the bouldery landslip of the **Fallen Rocks**. Two rivers have to be crossed using stepping stones on the way to the village of **Sannox**.

Day 5: Sannox to Brodick – 16km (10 miles)

There is little alternative to following the coastal road from **Sannox**, through the village of **Corrie**, and back to

Coillemore Point at the mouth of Loch Ranza near the village of Lochranza

Brodick. However, there is the option of climbing **Goat Fell** as a thrilling finale to the coastal walk, enabling the whole of the Isle of Arran to be seen before reaching the end of the walk. Refer to Walk 41 and Walk 1 for details about the paths from **Corrie** to the top of **Goat Fell** and down to **Brodick**. Once the Goat Fell path descends to **Cladach**, part of the main road can be avoided by using a path across the **golf course** to reach the **Arran Heritage Museum**, then a final stretch of road can be used to return to **Brodick** and the ferry terminal.

THE ARRAN COASTAL WAY

A specific Arran Coastal Way map is available, as well as an information leaflet. These can be obtained from the Tourist Information Centre at Brodick. Details about the route and its facilities, and details of packages that are available, including accommodation and baggage transfers, are available on the websites: **www.coastalway.co.uk** and **www.arrancoastalway.co.uk**.

APPENDIX 1
Gaelic/English Glossary

The oldest placenames on the Isle of Arran are Gaelic, since the language of earlier settlers is unknown. However, while the Gaelic culture was strong, it was also heavily influenced by Norse culture, and the most obvious placename legacies of that time are in the 'fell', 'gill' and 'dale' names. Gaelic placenames are often highly descriptive of landscape features, so a knowledge of the basic elements is useful, though centuries of change may mean that some of the features referred to are now redundant.

Abhainn – River
Allt – Stream
Ard – High
Ath – Ford
Auch – Field
Bal/Bally – Township
Ban/Bhan – White
Bealach – Pass/Col
Beag/Bheag – Small
Ben/Beinn/Bheinn – Mountain
Breac/Bhreac – Speckled
Biorach – Pointed
Buidhe – Yellow
Caillich – Old Woman/Witch
Caisteal – Castle
Caorach – Rowan Berries
Carn – Cairn
Ceum – Step
Cioch/Ciche – Breast
Cir/Chir – Comb/Crest
Clachan – Farm Hamlet
Cliabhain/Chliabhain – Cradle
Cnoc – Small Hill
Coire/Choire – Corrie
Coille – Wood

Creag – Crag
Dearg – Red
Donn – Brown
Dubh – Black
Dun – Fort
Eas – Waterfall
Eilean – Island
Fada/Fhada – Long
Fionn – Fair
Gaoithe – Wind
Garbh – Rough
Gearr – Sharp
Glais – Stream
Glas/Ghlas – Grey
Gleann – Glen/Valley
Guala – Shoulder
Iolaire – Eagle
Lagan – Hollow
Leac – Flat rock
Leathan – Broad
Loch – Lake
Lochan – Small Lake
Maol/Mhaoile – Bald
Meall – Rounded Hill
Mòr/Mhòr – Big

Mullach – Summit
Odhar – Dappled
Oighe – Youth
Reamhar – Fat
Righ – King

Ruadh – Russet
Suidhe – Seat
Torr – Small Hill
Uaine – Green
Uisge – Water

The pyramidal peak of Cir Mhòr requires hands-on scrambling to negotiate (Walk 43)

APPENDIX 2
Useful Contact Information

Tourist Information
Ayrshire and Arran Tourist Board, 15 Skye Road, Prestwick, KA9 2TA. ☎ 0845 2255121. Website **www.ayrshire-arran.com**. Email info@ayrshire-arran.com.
Tourist Information Centre, The Pier, Brodick, Isle of Arran, KA27 8AU. ☎ 01770 302140 or 302401.

Emergency Services
Emergency: dial 999 (or the European emergency number 112) to call the Police, Ambulance, Fire Service, Mountain Rescue or Coastguard.
Police Station, Lamlash, ☎ 01770 302573 for non-urgent matters.
Hospital, Lamlash, ☎ 01770 600777 for non-urgent matters.

Public Transport
Caledonian MacBrayne, Head Office, Ferry Terminal, Gourock, PA19 1QP. ☎ 08705 650000. Website **www.calmac.co.uk**. Email reservations@calmac.co.uk.
Caledonian MacBrayne, Ferry Terminal, Brodick, Isle of Arran. ☎ 01770 302166.
Holy Isle Ferry, The Pier, Lamlash, Isle of Arran. ☎ 01770 600998 or 600349, mobile 079327 86524.
Stagecoach Western Scottish bus services are contained in a timetable booklet that can be obtained on any bus on the Isle of Arran, or from the bus depot at the Ferry Terminal, or from the Tourist Information Centre in Brodick. *Postbus* services are also contained in the same timetable booklet. Websites **www.stagecoachbus.com/western** or **www.spt.co.uk**.
Traveline Scotland gives details of all public transport services in Scotland. ☎ 0870 6082608. Website **www.travelinescotland.com**.
Arran Heli-Tours, Tighbheag, Birchburn, Shiskine, Isle of Arran, KA27 8EP. ☎ 01770 860256 or 860326. Email neil@arranhelitours.fsnet.co.uk.

Access
Scottish Outdoor Access Code. Copies of the code are available from Scottish Natural Heritage and Tourist Information Centres.
Website **www.outdooraccess-scotland.com**.

Arran Access Trust, Membership Secretary, c/o NTS, Brodick Castle, Isle of Arran, KA27 8HY. ☎ 01770 302462. Website **www.arran-access-trust.org.uk**.
Isle of Arran Hillphone Service. ☎ 01770 302363. A recorded message alerting walkers to areas where deer stalking is taking place.

Scottish Natural Heritage
Scottish Natural Heritage, 12 Hope Terrace, Edinburgh, EH9 2AS.
☎ 0131 4474784. Website **www.snh.org.uk**. Email enquiries@snh.gov.uk.

National Trust for Scotland
National Trust for Scotland, Wemyss House, 28 Charlotte Square, Edinburgh, EH2 4ET. ☎ 0131 2439300. Website **www.nts.org.uk**. Email information@nts.org.uk.
National Trust for Scotland, Brodick Castle, Isle of Arran. ☎ 01770 302202. Email brodickcastle@nts.org.uk.
Countryside Ranger Service, Brodick Castle, Isle of Arran. ☎ 01770 302462. Rangers offer guided walks and organise events.

Forestry Commission
Forestry Commission Scotland, Silvan House, 231 Corstophine Road, Edinburgh, EH12 7AT. ☎ 0131 3340303. General public enquries 0845 3673787. Website **www.forestry.gov.uk/scotland**.
Forestry Enterprise, Auchrannie Road, Brodick, Isle of Arran, KA27 8BZ. ☎ 01770 302218. Forest rangers offer guided walks.

Arran Heritage Museum
Arran Heritage Museum, Rosaburn, Brodick, Isle of Arran. ☎ 01770 302636. Email arranmuseum@btinternet.com.

Arran Adventure Centre
Arran Adventure Centre, Brodick, Isle of Arran, KA27 8AJ. ☎ 01770 303907. Website **www.arranadventure.com**. Offers multiple outdoor activities.

Holy Island Project
Holy Island, Lamlash Bay, Isle of Arran, KA27 8GB. ☎ 01770 601100. Website **www.holyisland.org**.

Specialist Food and Drink
Arran Dairies, Market Road, Brodick.
Arran Chocolate Factory, Invercloy, Brodick.
Wooleys of Arran Bakery, Invercloy, Brodick.

Creelers Smokehouse, Cladach, Brodick.
Island Cheese Company, Cladach, Brodick.
Arran Brewery Company, Cladach, Brodick.
Arran Fine Foods, Old Mill, Lamlash.
Kingscross Herbs, Whiting Bay.
Torrylin Creamery, Kilmory.
Bellvue Creamery, Blackwaterfoot.
Isle of Arran Distillery, Lochranza.

Website **www.taste-of-arran.com** offers details of the 'Arran Taste Trail', or visit the Taste of Arran shop in Brodick to see most of the island's produce.

There is a good view across the Fairy Glenn to the mountains of northern Arran

LISTING OF CICERONE GUIDES

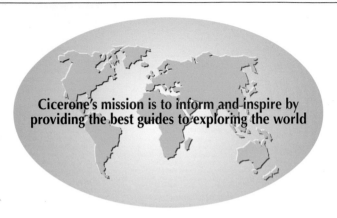

Cicerone's mission is to inform and inspire by providing the best guides to exploring the world

Since its foundation over 30 years ago, Cicerone has specialised in publishing guidebooks and has built a reputation for quality and reliability. It now publishes nearly 300 guides to the major destinations for outdoor enthusiasts, including Europe, UK and the rest of the world.

Written by leading and committed specialists, Cicerone guides are recognised as the most authoritative. They are full of information, maps and illustrations so that the user can plan and complete a successful and safe trip or expedition – be it a long face climb, a walk over Lakeland fells, an alpine traverse, a Himalayan trek or a ramble in the countryside.

With a thorough introduction to assist planning, clear diagrams, maps and colour photographs to illustrate the terrain and route, and accurate and detailed text, Cicerone guides are designed for ease of use and access to the information.

If the facts on the ground change, or there is any aspect of a guide that you think we can improve, we are always delighted to hear from you.

Cicerone Press
2 Police Square Milnthorpe Cumbria LA7 7PY
Tel:01539 562 069   Fax:01539 563 417
e-mail:info@cicerone.co.uk   web:www.cicerone.co.uk

CICERONE